December Light 1916

Kirk H. Neely

Illustrated by
Holly Barnett

Parson's Porch Books

www.parsonsporchbooks.com

December Light 1916
ISBN: Softcover 978-1-951472-45-0
Copyright © 2020 by Kirk H. Neely

This book is dedicated to the people of South Carolina, our state;

To the people of Spartanburg County, our home;

To the people of Georgetown County, where we vacationed for thirty-eight years;

And to eight congregations in Spartanburg County, South Carolina:

Morningside Baptist Church

Temple B'nai Israel

First Baptist Church, Spartanburg

First Presbyterian Church, Spartanburg

Palmetto Moravian Fellowship

First Presbyterian Church, Woodruff

Unitarian Universalist Church of Spartanburg

Saint Christopher's Episcopal Church

And to the congregation of

Knollwood Baptist Church,
Winston-Salem, North Carolina

Also by Kirk H. Neely

Where to Go for Help, with Wayne E. Oates

Comfort and Joy: Nine Stories for Christmas

When Grief Comes: Finding Strength for Today and Hope for Tomorrow

A Good Mule Is Hard to Find and Other Tales from Red Clay Country

Banjos, Barbecue, and Boiled Peanuts

Santa Almost Got Caught: Stories for Thanksgiving, Christmas, and the New Year

Neely Cousins

Hutson Heritage

By the Sea

Unto the Hills

Anthologies

Hub City Christmas

Stars Fell on Spartanburg

Outdoor Adventures in the Upcountry

And "By the Way,"

A weekly column published first by

The *H-J Weekly*

and now by

The Spartanburg *Herald-Journal*

www.kirkhneely.com

The North Island Light
Georgetown County, South Carolina

"Evhbody's a child of Gawd....

Evhbody jest want to be loved....

Gawd loves evhbody, even dem dat don't know hit....

De same light shine fo' evhbody"

Samuel Pringle
December Light 1916

TIDES

1.

Ankle deep in surf,
Low tide at dawn,
Gathering treasures.
Before my step,
      Shallow minnows scutter,
            Bright coquinas dig in.
Discarded bread bag in hand,
Searching for skeletal remains of the ocean's dead,
      Mollusks that left behind in the salty tide,
         Their spent pride,
            Shells of former selves,
Salt water and sand,
Washing and polishing the remains.
      Cockles,
         Clams,
            Calico scallops
               Find places in the sack.
Their cousins are preferred;
      Enfolded lettered olive,
         Coiled moon hell,
            Lobed baby's ear.
Perchance a whelk,
      Right-handed knobbed, with regal crown,
         Mirror image, left-handed lightning,
            Graceful channeled whelk.
Spying a knobby old whelk,
Thinking,
     Call him Lawrence,
       Lawrence Welk.
Laughing gulls,
      Excited by the prospect of bread,
         Hover overhead
            Laughing at me,
Too busy to notice,
      Seeking the dead among the living.

2.

Knee deep in seawater
High tide at midday,
Casting toward the jetty
     Pyramid sinker
          Double-hooked rig
               Fresh shrimp,
Watching, waiting.
     Surf rod high,
          Monofilament taut,
Watching, waiting,
For tap, tap, tug
Beneath the waves.
     One small spot
          One noisy croaker
               In the Sheetrock mud bucket

Watching, waiting
For something larger.
     Bottom-dwelling flounder,
          Rock-grazing sheepshead,
               Cruising bluefish.
Tap, tap, tug.
He's blue for sure
     Blue crab
          Eating the bait.
There's an idea!
     Eat the bait!
          Grill, boil, or fry the shrimp.
Watching, waiting,
An osprey circles
     Above and beyond the jetty.
          Plunging feet first,
Lifting on massive wings,
     With sharp talons,
          A fish larger
               Than I had imagined.

3.

Neck deep
In silent green,
    Beyond the breakers at dusk,
        Buoyed on rising tide.
Fading sunlight
    Reflecting glints
        Between dark peaks and valleys.
Looking east
    Toward Africa,
        Pondering the vastness,
Faint full moon,
    First stars,
    Final flight of brown pelicans.
Then, only yards away
    A splash!
        A mullet leaping for his life.
           As a dark dorsal fin
               Slices the sea.
Relief!
    A bottle-nosed dolphin
        Having supper.
Lifted by waves
    In the silent purple,
        One among many.
I am not alone.

Kirk H. Neely
Pawleys Island
July 2015

Timeline

*1874 – Eli Solomon is born.

**1881-1884 - Pogroms sweep southern Russia, including the Ukraine, leading to mass Jewish emigration. About 2 million Russian Jews emigrate in the period 1880-1920.

**1882 - The May Laws enacted by Czar Alexander III of Russia create a systematic policy of discrimination against Jews.

**1891 - The Congress of the United States eases immigration restrictions for Jews from the Russian Empire.

*1894 - Eli is married.

*1895 - Lenora is born.

*1896 - Fire destroys Eli Solomon's home in Odessa during a pogrom.

*1897 - Eli Solomon emigrates to America via Amsterdam and Canada.

*1898 – Eli lives with Uncle Mordecai in Georgetown and takes a job with Heiman Kaminski.

*1900 – Eli takes a job loading ships for the Atlantic Coast Lumber Company.

*1905 – Eli becomes a United States citizen.

*1906 – Eli becomes assistant lighthouse keeper at the North Island Lighthouse.

*1909 – Eli is promoted to lighthouse keeper at North Island.

**July 1914 – World War I begins.

*1916 – *December Light 1916* is set in December of 1916.

**April 1917 – United States enters World War I.

**1918-19 – Influenza pandemic infected 500 million people worldwide and killed upwards of 100 million people. The Spanish flu resulted in more than 3000 deaths in Georgetown County.

**November 1918 – Armistice ends World War I.

*1976 – Professor Rosen comes to the Lowcountry for a bicentennial lecture tour.

** Factual event

* Fictional event

DECEMBER 1916

Su	Mo	Tu	We	Th	Fr	Sa
					1	2
3	4	5	6	7	8	9
10	11	12	13	14	15	16
17	18	19	20	21	22	23
24	25	26	27	28	29	30
31						

25 Christmas Day

19-26 Hanukkah (Each day begins at sundown.)

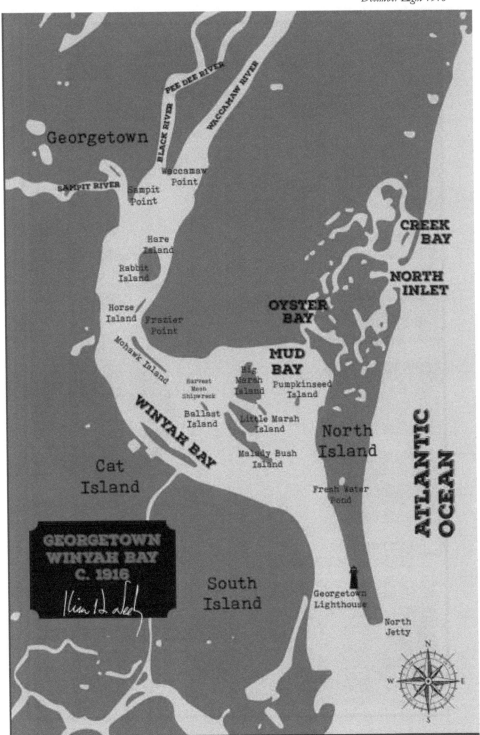

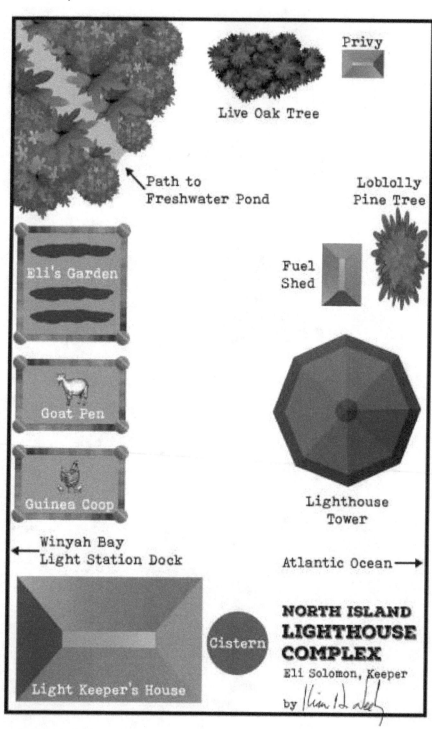

Live Oak Tree

Privy

Path to
Freshwater Pond

Loblolly
Pine Tree

Fuel
Shed

Eli's Garden

Goat Pen

Guinea Coop

Lighthouse
Tower

Winyah Bay
Light Station Dock

Atlantic Ocean →

Cistern

NORTH ISLAND LIGHTHOUSE COMPLEX

Eli Solomon, Keeper

by

Light Keeper's House

Prologue

Dr. Lenora Rosen gazed out of the window of Row 21 as the jet neared the Holy City, Charleston, South Carolina. In the distance, she thought she spied the steeple of St. Philip's Episcopal Church. She traced the course of the Ashley River, hoping to catch a glimpse of the Atlantic Ocean, but the haze over Charleston Harbor blocked her view.

Below her, the retired professor saw the airport. The crowded runway congested with an array of fire trucks, ambulances, and police vehicles, all with lights flashing. Workers were spraying thick white foam on the tarmac.

Just then, in a deceptively calm voice, the pilot spoke to the passengers, "Ladies and gentlemen, we are making our approach into the Charleston airport. We have a mechanical problem with our landing mechanism. Emergency vehicles will be standing by. The landing strip has been sprayed with fire retardant foam to ensure our safety. This might get rough. Do exactly as your crew instructs you to do."

Then came a voice, business-like, "Ladies and gentlemen, this is your flight attendant. Make sure all serving trays and personal possessions are properly stored. Your seats should be in the upright position. Keep your feet on the floor. If you have a pillow, place it across your knees. Bend forward with your head in your lap. Hold on tight while we make our final descent."

The distinguished professor emeritus, an elderly woman sitting next to the window in row 21, thought to herself, *Wouldn't it be better not to use the words final descent?*

She followed the instructions exactly. Leaning forward onto the pillow in her own lap, she was grateful that she had been faithfully doing her flexibility exercises.

The aircraft whined as it dropped toward the tarmac. The big jet engines roared to slow the plane. The rear wheels lowered into position; the front wheels did not. The aircraft touched down with a bump as the rear wheels made contact, then a loud thud as the belly flopped to the pavement. The jet skidded on the foam-covered runway, finally sliding to a stop when the nose hit the soft grassy knoll at the end of the landing strip.

"Welcome to Charleston, South Carolina. Thank you for flying with us today. We sincerely apologize for any inconvenience. We will have ground transportation take you to the terminal where one of our customer service representatives will meet with you."

Wouldn't it be better if they didn't call it a terminal? the woman on Row 21 asked herself as she sat up and fussed with her hair. She found her glasses on the floor, unbroken, and put them back on. Standing in the aisle, she straightened her clothing, before disembarking from the aircraft.

It was December 1976. At the invitation of the Southern Jewish Historical Society, the distinguished lady in Row 21 had come to Charleston for several speaking engagements. A vibrant and courageous woman, Dr. Rosen was an internationally known scholar in the History of Judaism in Eastern Europe. She had graduated from the University of South Carolina and then earned her Ph.D. at Brandeis University. She had been encouraged by the Jewish community in

Georgetown to pursue her education and had received a nominal scholarship from the Southern Jewish Historical Society. Most of her education was funded by her work and by an anonymous benefactor. She was among the first female faculty members of Hebrew Union College in Cincinnati, Ohio, where she made her home.

Now Professor Rosen was returning to South Carolina for the bicentennial celebration. She had a carefully prepared manuscript, and she intended to give the same address in three different venues. The title of her speech was "Hanukkah and the Blessings of Liberty."

She presented two addresses in Charleston on Wednesday. The first, a morning convocation at the College of Charleston, was poorly attended. The second was delivered that evening to a packed house at Kahal Kadosh Beth Elohim, the second oldest Jewish synagogue in the United States.

The slender eighty-one-year-old teacher was to conclude her visit to South Carolina with an address at Congregation Beth Elohim in Georgetown on Thursday, December 16, the first night of Hanukkah.

After Thursday lunch with the women of Hadassah, Dr. Rosen traveled with her host couple along Highway 17 from Charleston to Georgetown. When the late model Buick sedan crossed the Cooper River Bridge, the smell of salt air and the expanse of the water flowing out toward the Atlantic brought a flood of distant but pleasant memories.

North of Mt. Pleasant the professor asked if they might stop at one of the many sweetgrass basket stands along the roadside. Dr. Rosen knew these carefully crafted baskets were a traditional Gullah art form. She wanted to purchase one for her home in Cincinnati.

A basketmaker named Harriet had fashioned her offerings from local sweetgrass, pine needles, and palmetto fronds. Dr. Rosen admired

Harriet's work and purchased a basket. The professor especially enjoyed conversing with the ebony woman who spoke in a soft Gullah accent. Hearing Harriet's voice brought back more fond memories.

As the black sedan continued north through Awendaw, Professor Rosen sat in the rear seat, fumbling with a manuscript. She had delivered her bicentennial address, "Hanukkah and the Blessings of Liberty," twice in Charleston. She had notes for a second presentation that she had outlined for the Georgetown audience. She barely glanced at the papers in her lap. She knew them well.

Instead, she gazed at the blue sky and the deep December-green forest along the highway. A grove of live oaks, draped in Spanish moss, shaded an unpainted heart pine farmhouse. A trio of turkey buzzards picked at the remains of a roadkilled raccoon. To the east, in the distance, a red-tailed hawk soared effortlessly on the afternoon breeze blowing in from the Atlantic.

Crossing the twin bridges over the blackwaters of the South and North Santee Rivers, the Buick entered Georgetown County. The third oldest city in South Carolina, following Charleston and Beaufort,

Georgetown was founded in 1729 and became an official port of entry in 1732. The black sedan descended into the city from the high bridge on US Highway 17. The offensive odor of the paper mill was inescapable.

Dr. Rosen made a decision. She would use some of the information from her prepared address for Charleston. Still, she intended to use her outline for a Hanukkah story to share with Congregation Beth Elohim, a true story that had occurred six decades before, in 1916.

When she arrived at the Temple, she was surprised to see a large gathering. She was greeted by Rabbi Rubin and by the president of the congregation. "We don't usually have this many for Friday night services," the president said, "But tonight we have many non-Jews from the community who have joined us for this special Hanukkah observance." Those attending included a cross-section of Georgetown residents, Jews and Christians, Black and white.

Dr. Rosen looked at the program. There were not that many preliminaries before she was to speak. Her announced topic was printed in the bulletin. When the time came for the introduction of the speaker, Rabbi Rubin made it clear that he did not know Professor Rosen personally. His words were stiff and lengthy.

After expressions of gratitude and greeting, Dr. Rosen began to tell a story from sixty years in the past.

Chapter One

Professor Rosen:

The Georgetown Lighthouse stands on North Island near the mouth of Winyah Bay. The beacon is inaccessible by road. Because it is thirteen miles over water from the port, most residents of Georgetown have never seen the lighthouse. Only on the darkest nights can the townsfolk see the faint sweep of the beam.

Rich in diverse, sometimes vicious, wildlife, the island was a forbidding place. In 1916, the time this account takes place, North Island was inhabited only by the lighthouse keeper and perhaps one other person. Only rarely did other humans visit these secluded shores.

Saturday, December 9, 1916

The half-moon gave an eerie glow to the beach along the Winyah Bay side of North Island. The outgoing flow slowed as it moved toward the twin jetties where it emptied into the Atlantic Ocean. A dinghy drifted in the slack water. Voices whispered across the water. Muffled laughs mingled as oars dipped into the green bay. At ebb tide, the small boat dropped anchor in the shallows down the shore away from the dock near the lighthouse.

Every fifteen seconds, the lighthouse beam crossed the bay sweeping back toward Georgetown. Between the passes of the light, stars danced in the December sky.

Quietly two shadowy figures left the boat and waded through the cool water. One had pant cuffs rolled up to the knees. The other lifted a dress skirt above the thighs. The two walked hand in hand further down the beach behind a dune hidden from the bright light circling high overhead. Just above the waterline, bare feet crunched through the bed of broken shells.

The two shadows, one a slender male form, the other a full-figured female shape, paused for a passionate kiss. Their embrace grew more intense.

They hastily disrobed, haphazardly tossing their clothing in a heap on the sand. Completely stripped bare, they held each other close, gently lowering to the cool, wet sand, bodies entwined. Perspiration and damp sand clung to their skin as breathless passion increased.

Suddenly they stopped.

One of them became aware that they were being watched. Startled, they sat up. They glimpsed a frightening sight, faintly illuminated by the moon. Standing at the crest of the dune above them was a being whose skin was as black as coal. His hair and beard were as white as cotton. The ghostly vision stared with piercing eyes that gleamed in the moonlight.

The lovers jumped to their feet, cursing in shock and terror. Grabbing their clothing, they ran back up the beach to the waiting dinghy. A dog barked in the distance. A bird made a raucous sound from a treetop. Still naked, the couple threw their jumbled garments into the boat, hoisted the anchor, and pushed out into the current of the incoming tide of Winyah Bay.

Now headed to Georgetown, they looked back toward the dunes. There was no sign of the looming apparition who had startled them.

As they dressed, they realized that an article of clothing was missing. On the shore of North Island, floating in the gentle waves of the rising tide in Winyah Bay, a woman's lacey undergarment slowly settled in the shallow water.

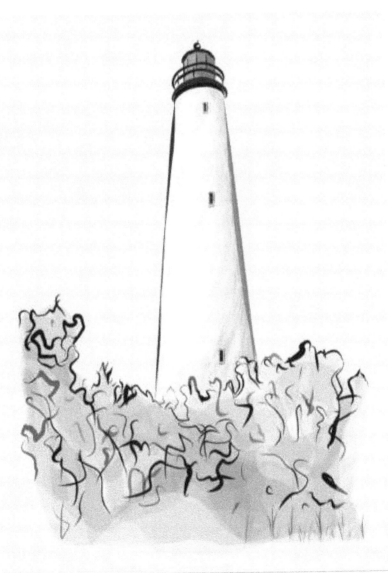

Chapter Two

Professor Rosen:

When the first Jewish settlers arrived in Georgetown, the area's economy was dominated by planters. Abraham and Solomon Cohen moved from Charleston to Georgetown in the early 1760s. Sons of Rabbi Moses Cohen of Charleston's synagogue, Kahal Kadosh Beth Elohim, they had emigrated from London with their father in 1750. Mordecai Myers arrived in Georgetown at about the same time. All three became successful merchants and men of prominence.

The Jewish population grew significantly in the decades after the Cohens and Myers arrived. It is believed that by 1800, about 80 Jews, roughly ten percent of the white population, lived in the town, making it one of the oldest and the second-largest Jewish community in South Carolina, after Charleston.

Georgetown Jews rallied behind the Confederacy once the Civil War broke out. Five who died fighting for the South are buried in the Jewish cemetery here. After the war, Heiman Kaminski settled in Georgetown and opened a dry goods store with his brother-in-law, Sol Emanuel. From his modest start, Kaminski became one of the most prosperous and influential citizens of Georgetown.

Shabbes, the Sabbath, observances were held in a room located above a local jewelry store on Front Street. Jews in Georgetown traveled to Charleston for High Holy Days until Temple Beth Elohim was founded in Georgetown in 1904.

Kaminski and other Jews were primary figures in the growth of the town in the latter half of the nineteenth century. They encouraged modernization by extending rail lines, opening communications, and supporting other economic enterprises.

Jews were an integral part of Georgetown. They prepared the way for immigrant Jews from Eastern Europe. Eli Solomon was one of those immigrants.

Saturday, December 16, 1916

The fire raged against the black Ukrainian night, engulfing in flames the small wooden home in the Odessa ghetto.

Just before dawn every morning, they blazed again in the nightmares of the lighthouse keeper. Eli Solomon was panic-stricken before he awakened abruptly, sweating and weeping, from his fretful sleep. Each night as he rolled his weary body into his hammock, his tortured soul dreaded the nightmares that were the constant prelude to his day.

The details of the recurring dreams were vague as if the scenes were being viewed through thick ocean fog. The night terrors were persistent. And, there was always fire, the fire that took his wife and young daughter from him.

Eli removed the cotton sheet and the wool blanket, swinging his legs from the hammock. He planted his cracked bare feet onto the cold pine floor. The large reddish-brown dog, sleeping near the wood stove, stirred, stretched, and yawned. Dog and man walked together to the door and out onto the front porch. The dark December Saturday morning was still. The faint howl of red wolves rose from the distant thicket up the island. Every fifteen seconds, a shaft of light, the beam from the beacon, swept the horizon and back above the house. In the intervals, a sliver of moonlight reflected across the waves breaking gently on the white sand at the water's edge.

The dog loped down the wooden steps to the edge of the yard. From his roost atop a nearby live oak, a guinea cock sounded the alarm. The dog ignored the squawking as he trotted across the sandy yard. Lifting his hind leg at his usual place, the dog sprayed a half-dead yaupon shrub.

Eli removed the lid of a large empty pickle jar and relieved himself. Steam rose into the cool air as the warm liquid flowed into the glass container. He twisted the lid securely in place, reserving the urine for later use.

Back in the house, Eli took three sticks of heart pine and several pieces of live oak from a wooden box behind the stove. He rekindled the fire in the stove and prepared a pot of coffee, placing it on the cooking surface.

While the coffee percolated, he dressed. The calendar on the wall indicated that it was Saturday, December 16, 1916. Eli put on his clothes, denim jeans and a denim shirt. A duplicate set hung on a peg near the hammock that was suspended in the corner of the large room. Every Friday afternoon, just before the Sabbath sundown, he took a bath and changed into clean clothes, washing jeans, pants, socks, and underwear in the bathwater before using the same water to mop the pine floors.

Still barefooted, Eli poured a tin cup of black coffee, adding a spoonful of sugar. Again, he walked out on to the front porch. In the quiet, dark morning, he nursed his hot drink. This was the best time of the day for Eli. The dread of the nightmares had passed. The day was before him. These moments before dawn were his most peaceful. The beating of his heart synchronized with the rhythm of the waves on the calm sea. He breathed the salt air deeply, sipped the steaming coffee, and allowed himself to find blessed peace, momentary *shalom*.

As the lighthouse keeper on North Island, Eli Solomon lived a solitary life. He had been at his post for seven years. A Jewish immigrant from the Ukraine, he was fortunate to have the job, and it suited him well. He was a man of medium height and weight who was physically strong for his size. His curly black hair was tinged with gray. Though most Orthodox Jewish men traditionally kept long curly locks known as *peyos,* these were not required by the Torah. What was required was that the sideburns be unshaven.

Sideburns and a beard framed Eli's weathered and suntanned face. Black, thick eyebrows arched toward his strong, bent nose, previously broken in a Ukrainian street fight when he was a youth. His heavy brows hooded his dark eyes, eyes that revealed a capacity for gratitude and compassion, as well as an inner strength that gave him the courage of his convictions.

Powerful calloused hands and sore feet were marks of his harsh environment. Eli dipped a sea sponge into the jar of urine and applied the amber liquid to his cracked feet and chapped hands, a time-honored remedy he learned from his grandfather in the Ukraine. When his hands and feet were air-dried, he removed a tube of lanolin from his shirt pocket. He rubbed the thick grease into the cracks of his feet. He put on his socks and returned to the house to wash his hands before applying lanolin to them.

As the Sabbath dawn approached, a great horned owl hooted one final time from a yellow pine tree at the edge of the woods. Guinea fowl stirred from their roost in a live oak. The dog ambled down the path through the trees toward the house. In his mouth, he proudly carried a mallard drake. The dog presented the limp duck to Eli.

He praised the dog, speaking in Yiddish. "Good work, Melchizedek. The duck will be our supper."

The dog moved closer, panting from his hunt. Eli scratched his ears and examined the animal for ticks and debris. Removing a sandspur from a front paw, he patted the large dog again, speaking words of appreciation in the Yiddish language from his hometown, Odessa.

The dog trotted away for his next adventure. At first light, Eli put on his worn boots and lifted a cloth bag from a peg near the door. Before returning to the porch, Eli retrieved a handful of dried corn from a wooden bin located beneath the open shelves that served as a pantry. Even though it was the Sabbath, the lighthouse keeper walked across the firm sand to his work.

As he walked, the first guinea, a cock, flew from the live oak tree landing at his feet. Eli paused, tossing a few kernels of dried corn to the ground. Soon the other guinea fowl descended, scurrying around his feet. Eli scattered the corn, making sure each speckled bird received a ration. Between the abundant insects and the dried seed heads, the flock of guineas had plenty to eat. Eli used the corn to keep the guineas close to the property and to coax the hens into a crude shelter during the spring egg-laying season.

He took a detour on his route to the light tower over to the oak tree from which the guinea had flown. There on the ground beneath the tree, he found a guinea fowl sitting on a nest of oak leaves and pine needles. The warm December weather had confused a guinea hen. Her keets would never survive this late in the year.

He retrieved the four eggs from the nest and took them to the kitchen in the keeper's house. The mother hen joined the rest of the flock pecking at the corn.

The thin clouds over the Atlantic Ocean brightened with purple, pink, and orange swirls. The rising sun sliced through the faint line separating sky from sea. As the red orb climbed above the horizon, Eli ascended the circular stairway of the Georgetown Lighthouse.

Every dawn for the last seven years, Eli had climbed the 124 stone steps, winding his way to the round lantern room at the top of the eighty-seven-foot tower. He extinguished the light, snuffing out the burning wicks.

His first official task of the day completed, Eli paused for a moment to gaze out of the large windows. The sun was high enough now to cast shafts of light through the broken clouds. The light reflected off the calm ocean, creating a gleaming path through the waves from the blue horizon to the white beach. A flight of brown pelicans glided above the surf, searching for mullet just beyond the breakers. Further out, a small pod of bottle-nosed dolphins arched through the waves, feeding as they swam. Noisy herring gulls hovered, scavenging the leftovers.

In the lantern room atop the lighthouse, Eli reached into the cloth bag slung over his shoulder and replaced his seaman's cap with a well-used skullcap. He wrapped his tasseled prayer shawl around his shoulders. He fastened phylacteries on his forehead and his left forearm. Gently swaying, bending forward and back in the typical manner of Jewish prayer, Eli began chanting in Hebrew to greet the day, "Blessed art thou Lord, our God, King of the Universe."

Adding a few more sentences in Yiddish, he completed the morning devotion. He removed the phylacteries from his forearm and forehead; his yarmulke, the skullcap; and his tallith, the prayer shawl, returning them to the cloth bag.

The lantern room of the lighthouse had become Eli's place of prayer, both morning and evening. He could not attend the synagogue in Georgetown thirteen miles away, especially on *Shabbes*. It was Eli's constant dilemma. How to be a devout Jew and meet the demands of life as a lighthouse keeper?

How to follow the regulations of the United States Lighthouse Service and live as an observant Jew?

Eli descended the stone stairway to the tabby floor below. At the door, he was met by Melchizedek, his trusted companion, and, other than God, the only being with whom he spoke daily. He had always wanted to become proficient in Hebrew, but other than the memorized prayers, he spoke to both God and dog in his mother tongue, Ukrainian, or in Yiddish.

"Come, let's have breakfast."

The man and his dog walked to the keeper's house. Eli kicked off his boots on the porch, touched the handcrafted cedar *mezuzah* as he opened the door, and hung the cloth bag, his official cap, and his coat on pegs inside the house. The warmth from the wood-burning stove drew the man and the dog to the kitchen.

He broke a fresh loaf of bread, cut several chunks from a large wheel of sharp cheddar cheese, sat at the table, and said the blessing, praising God, the one "who brings forth bread from the earth."

Other than making coffee, Eli did not cook on *Shabbes*, but today he would violate that portion of Torah law. The duck fetched by his dog, Melchizedek, would be their evening meal. There was no refrigeration on North Island. Meat had to be heavily salted or quickly cooked lest it spoil. The thought of breaking the Sabbath bothered Eli, but there was no reasonable alternative.

The mallard would be for supper. The midday meal was sparse but tasty. He put an equal amount of cheese in a bowl for the dog and on his own plate. They ate together in silence.

After the meal, Eli cleaned the dog's bowl and filled it with fresh water. He poured coffee in a tin cup, added sugar, and sat near the woodstove, watching as the embers burned low. Melchizedek lapped the water and settled beside the man. Eli scratched the animal's ears and admired the dog. He was a mixed breed, part shepherd, part retriever, and maybe other parts as well. He had the best qualities of all of his ancestors. He was a natural hunter and herder.

Melchizedek was the faithful protector of the lighthouse keeper, a flock of guineas, and five Nubian goats, a buck, and two does, and a pair of kids. His bark warned when the island's red wolves or black bears were near and directed the goats out of harm's way.

The dog had come from nowhere. While just a pup with large feet, he arrived one day as Eli was gathering wild duck eggs. Eli named him for the priest of Salem, who mysteriously appeared before Abraham. Occasionally, the dog would disappear for a day or two. Eli suspected his companion had sired several litters among the wild dogs and red wolves that roamed North Island.

Eli took a worn book from the table near the chair and read from the scriptures. He concluded with a brief prayer from Psalm 24. He read from another equally tattered book, *The Pink Book*, the 1902 edition of regulations issued by the United States Lighthouse Service. Eli made a habit of reading a section of both books every day.

Eli found a large pan on the kitchen shelf and a sharp knife in the drawer. Taking his cap from the peg, Eli walked onto the porch to put on his boots. Then, man and dog went to work. The guineas scurried about the sandy yard using their soft voices, "Buckwheat, buckwheat." Eli unlatched the gate to the goat pen. Melchizedek accompanied the Nubians out to the dunes to graze.

Eli went into the yard to clean the duck, a clear violation of the Sabbath, but he couldn't let the duck spoil. That would be foolish. He made short work of the task. As he prepared the bird, he admired the colorful feathers.

In the bird kingdom, the males are endowed with more beauty than the females. Not so for humans, he thought.

He recalled the beauty of his young wife, her dark eyes, her glowing skin, her flowing black hair, the curve of her neck, the shape of her body, her lips.

Eli chased the memories from his mind. He knew full well that they would return unbidden.

He placed the dressed duck in the pan. The customary way of kashering fowl, making the duck kosher, was to salt it, but his allotment of salt was depleted until he could be resupplied by the lighthouse tender boat. So, he walked to the ocean, filled the pan with salt water, and returned to the house. He would soak the duck in the cool brine for several hours to remove excess blood. It would be ready to cook in the afternoon. The Sabbath ended at sundown. Eli planned to enjoy the mallard for supper. Of course, he intended to share with his dog.

Eli retrieved the glass jar of urine from the porch. His vegetable garden was located on a small rise above the house near the edge of the woods. He had spent much time and energy preparing and cultivating the small patch of ground. The location made it vulnerable to vegetarian animals.

Cottontail rabbits and whitetail deer that roamed the island were especially interested in Eli's agricultural efforts. The guineas kept insect pests at bay. The dog did a good job of herding the goats away from the plot as well as discouraging other encroachers. The goats were penned at night, and Melchizedek was usually inside the keeper's house.

After his daily foot care, Eli then used his own urine to keep the nocturnal herbivores away. Marking his territory, he sprinkled each morning's output around the perimeter of his garden. It was not a fail-safe solution, but the scent of a human was a repellent for most animals.

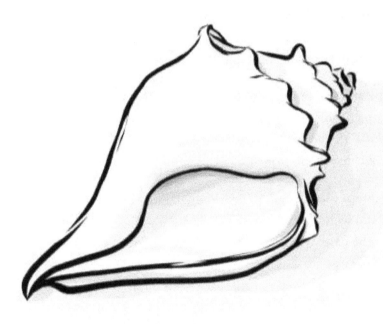

Eli walked a narrow path through the dunes to the bay side of the island. Stooping at the water's edge, a battered knobbed whelk, half-buried in the sand, caught his eye. He rinsed the shell in the gentle surf admiring the simple beauty of the discarded old mollusk shell. Then,

Eli washed the pickle jar and the sea sponge in the water of Winyah Bay before returning them to the porch. He placed the newly found seashell with the others in his collection on the windowsill inside the keeper's house.

Eli walked back across the sandy yard to resume his duties. At the oil shed, Eli unlocked the door. Lighthouse Service regulations regarding the oil supply were particularly stringent. As a precaution, the small building was separated from the other structures in the complex. The oil shed had a single purpose – to safeguard the supply of kerosene used to fuel the massive light atop the tower. The five-gallon cans were marked Lighthouse Oil printed beneath the Texaco Star.

Along with other supplies, the kerosene was delivered every three months by the tender ship from the Lighthouse Service. The kerosene was packed in wooden boxes, four cans to the crate. Eli lifted one of the square cans by the handle and relocked the oil shed.

From the storeroom, he gathered a wooden box, an oil case modified with a rope handle. The box held the daily supplies needed to maintain the light. With the box in one hand and the can of kerosene in the other, Eli climbed the stone stairs to the top of the tower.

In the lantern room atop the lighthouse, he began a daily routine. He washed and wiped soot from the glass chimney on the brass lamp. He polished the base of the lamp, trimmed the two wicks, and refilled the base with kerosene. The lamp, which held a quart and a half of oil, burned about four ounces of fuel each hour. During December, when the nights were long and the days short, it took a full lamp of oil to keep the light burning from dusk to dawn.

Setting the lamp aside, Eli cleaned the large bulls-eye lens and the curved prismatic lens above and below the center lens in each of the four panels. The entire configuration was a fourth-order Fresnel lens.

The large lens looked to Eli like a glass beehive. As he cleaned each panel, he thought of the Frenchman Augustin Fresnel, the inventor of the lens. *What a remarkable accomplishment! Focusing and magnifying the light of a single lamp into a concentrated beam that could pierce the darkness eighteen miles out into the ocean.*

Eli replaced the lamp inside the lens, then dusted and oiled the clockwork mechanism that rotated the lens. As he wound the steel line that held the large torpedo-shaped weight, he examined it for wear. The light operated just like a grandfather clock. The weight drove the large gears that were governed to rotate the light one complete turn every minute, causing the light to sweep the horizon every fifteen seconds.

Eli pulled the keeper's watch from his pocket. Regulations required that he complete daily maintenance in the lantern room before 10:00 A.M. He was twelve minutes ahead of schedule.

Eli took a moment to enjoy the view on this gorgeous Saturday morning. In the crook of the north jetty, Eli watched as an osprey lifted a large mullet from the sea. The bird carrying its catch in its talons flew to the tall loblolly pine near the oil shed. He saw the large bird fishing almost every morning, taking her catch to the highest branches of the stately pine. Even though he knew the tree was a favorite perch for the graceful raptor, Eli had requested permission to remove the tree, fearing that, in a storm, it might fall, damaging the building. Inspector Roy Holden had denied his request, reminding him that the regulations did not allow for the removal of trees. Officer Holden denied most of the requests of lighthouse keeper Eli Solomon.

Descending the curved stairway, Eli noticed several places where the paint on the railing had chipped. It was just the kind of thing that Inspector Holden would yell about. Roy Holden always found something to scream about.

Eli returned the supply box and the fuel can to the storeroom.

The lighthouse keeper spent the remainder of the morning walking the government property. He checked the goat pen where the goats were kept each night. He also examined the smaller guinea pen though it would not be used again until the guineas laid fertile eggs and hatched their young. Then the pen was necessary to keep the brooding nest in a safe place and to protect the baby keets after they hatched.

He had constructed both enclosures with driftwood found on the beaches along federal property bordering Winyah Bay and the Atlantic Ocean. He had added chicken wire to the guinea pen.

As he surveyed the property, Eli took note of several things that needed his attention. Keeping a lighthouse required constant maintenance. It was always a work in progress.

Inside the keeper's house, Eli stoked the fire in the stove. He drained Melchizedek's mallard of brine and blood. He stuffed the duck's cavity with a diced onion and several rosemary twigs from the garden. He placed the prepared bird in a cast-iron Dutch oven and positioned it on the cooking surface. Gathering hot coals from the stove into a dustpan, he placed the glowing embers on the Dutch oven lid. He left the duck to cook until dusk.

Back outside, the warm day felt more like summer than winter. It had been an unusual year with five major storms. By December, ocean storms should have ended. But the sea is unpredictable, like a capricious woman. Eli knew that the still air and the calm water were signs that somewhere in the Atlantic, bad weather was brewing.

Eli checked the water level in the underground cistern. It provided fresh water for drinking, bathing, and cleaning. He lowered a bucket into the dark vat and raised the pail only half-filled with water. He sipped the cool liquid, quenching his own thirst. The goats and Melchizedek needed water, too. Eli gave a whistle that was clear and shrill.

In the distance, Melchizedek barked and moved the goats to Eli. With collar bells ringing, the stately Nubians walked in single file. The young drank first, followed by the does, then the buck, and finally the dog.

Tomorrow they would travel up the island to the freshwater pond where they could drink their fill. Today, though, the bucket only half full would be their ration. The unusually warm, dry weather had forced Eli to conserve cistern water. To make sure the animals had enough to drink, he had to take them to the freshwater pond a mile away.

Toward day's end, the guineas began to scatter, flying to roost in the trees along the edge of the woods. One single feather drifted slowly to the ground. Eli stooped to pick it up, admiring the delicate form and striking markings on the small treasure.

The dominant male guinea fowl flew to the highest perch, as the lighthouse keeper climbed the spiral staircase of the lighthouse to say his evening prayers.

Then, using official Lighthouse Service matches, he lit the twin lamp and released the torpedo weight. The heavy lens turned, casting a strong rhythmic beam eighteen miles across the Atlantic and back over Winyah Bay.

Inside the house, Eli lit the kerosene lamp. The duck was ready to be eaten for supper. After the blessing, the man and the dog enjoyed every morsel. Eli complimented the dog on his choice of game fowl. After the dishes were clean, Eli moved the lamp from the center of the table so he could read a few passages from the Torah. Then, he extinguished the lamp and rolled into his hammock.

He heard a red wolf howl in the distance. The dog turned his ears without moving. An owl hooted from the edge of the woods. The island needed rain. Eli knew that rain would come. It always did.

Chapter Three

Professor Rosen:

In Georgetown County, four rivers flow into Winyah Bay – the Black, the Pee Dee, the Waccamaw, and the Sampit. This was a prime area for the development of large plantations through land grants from the King of England.

By 1721 the petition for a new parish, Prince George, Winyah, on the Black River, was granted. In 1729, Elisha Screven laid the plan for Georgetown. He developed the city in a four-by-eight block grid, now referred to as the Historic District. It still includes many of the original homes.

Soon after Georgetown was established, indigo became the cash crop with rice as a secondary crop. The Winyah Indigo Society opened and maintained the first public school between Charles Town and Wilmington.

Before the American Revolution, Georgetown sent both Thomas Lynch, Sr. and Thomas Lynch, Jr. to Philadelphia, Pennsylvania, to sign the Declaration of Independence. During the final years of the conflict, Georgetown was the critical port for supplying General Nathanael Greene's army. The Swamp Fox, General Francis Marion, led many battles in this area.

Following the American Revolution, rice became the staple crop. It required the low land along the rivers for cultivation. Seventy rice plantations were established around Georgetown on its four rivers. By 1840, Georgetown County produced nearly one-half of the total rice grown in the United States. Georgetown exported more rice than any other port in the world.

The rice plantations of Georgetown County were carved out of tidal swamps along coastal rivers by slaves brought to South Carolina from West Africa. Slaves from Senegal, Gambia, Angola, and Sierra Leone were the most valued by Georgetown planters because they came from rice-growing regions. With primitive tools, the slaves cleared the low-lying swampland of cypress and gum trees. They built canals, dikes, and irrigation trunks that allowed the flooding and draining of fields with the high and low tides. From the eighteenth century to the time of the Civil War, slaves planted, tended, and harvested the rice crops that made plantation owners wealthy. By 1860 and the beginning of the Civil War, there were more than 18,000 slaves in Georgetown County.

After the Civil War and the Emancipation Proclamation, many of the freed African-Americans settled along the Atlantic Coast of South Carolina and Georgia and their sea islands. These freed slaves were bound together by a unique language and way of life known as Gullah.

Gullah is a personal and community identity. The soft Gullah dialect mixes English as spoken in the Deep South with West African languages. For example, the word "you" becomes "oonuh" in Gullah. The Gullah people cherish their traditions that continue in their arts and crafts, in their soul food and in their soul music, in their folklore and their folk songs, and in their religion and their spiritual awareness. Samuel Pringle was a former slave, and he was Gullah.

Saturday, December 16, 1916, continued

Bumpy as a washboard, the rutted sandy track that followed the bank of the Sampit River meandered among live oak trees draped with Spanish moss. Black families, the sons and daughters of former slaves from the plantations of Georgetown County, had settled beneath the massive trees. The modest dwellings along the Gullah Line were constructed from rough-hewn heart pine. Most of the houses were unpainted except for the blue doorframes. Two or three were painted blue all over, haint blue, the Gullah people called it. The color was said to keep evil spirits away.

In the freshly swept yard outside his unpainted shanty, Samuel Pringle sat on a heart pine log bench in the shade of a live oak tree. The Spanish moss clinging to the branches of the aged tree hung almost motionless in the dry December air. There had been no rain since before Thanksgiving. The weather had been unusually warm.

Samuel removed his sweat-stained felt hat, dropping it on the bench beside him. Using an old faded bandana, he mopped his glistening bald head and brow.

Some said this hot December weather was a sign of the end times. The preacher on the street corner in Georgetown had said so on this very day. "We are living in the last days. Jesus is coming again," he shouted. "And not as a baby in a manger this time. The trumpet will sound, and the graves will be open. This time there'll be fire from on high."

Samuel didn't know about the end times. His thought was that if the reverend wasn't huffing and panting and blowing so much hot air, the weather might turn cooler.

Samuel's large, strong hands whittled a piece of red cedar. He had cut a cedar tree from the rise above the river and given it to John Howard and his family for Christmas last year. After Christmas, John had cut the branches off and used them for kindling. But he saved the tree trunk for Samuel, thinking the cedar would make a suitable walking stick for a crippled man. But the leftover Christmas tree was a little too tall, so Samuel had cut ten inches or so off the thick end. The leftover butt was too good to burn, so he kept it until later.

He had used the walking stick every day for nearly a year, but he had saved that piece off the bottom to carve something. Now, this year Sally Howard wanted a doll for Christmas. There was no money to buy a doll, so Samuel had decided to spend what was left of Saturday afternoon on the task of carving a doll for Sally from the butt end of last year's Christmas tree.

With his sharpened jackknife, he peeled thin strips of bark from the dry stick he held in his gnarled left hand. When the bark was removed, Samuel paused to enjoy the fragrance released from the cedar even a year after it had been cut. He examined the pattern of the grain and imagined the female figure that would emerge from the wood.

He thought of the fine shape of Maggie Howard. Samuel enjoyed sitting on his front porch and watching Maggie hang laundry on the clothesline. Even a slight breeze made her faded cotton dress cling to her curves.

He thought of his own wife, Rachel, and the rhyme she would say when she saw him looking at another woman.

De good Lawd made women fo' a man to see,

and ever' woman knows 'tis so.

Oonuh can look all you want, but 'member dis,

when it come to touchin',

Oonuh best be touchin' me.

Remembering the rhyme made Samuel chuckle to himself.

Rachel had been gone for three years. Remembering her was bittersweet for Samuel. She was only sixteen when they were married. Miz Pringle wanted them to have a Christian wedding at Chicora Wood, so they repeated their vows standing before the priest who came out from All Saints Episcopal Church. Then, following a tradition among the slaves, they stepped over a broom together to seal their promise.

Being married to Rachel made Samuel feel like he had finally found freedom. She was the most handsome woman he had ever seen and the smartest, too. She knew how to parse and cipher even before they got married. She had taught him numbers and a little reading. After supper, she read to him from the Good Book and taught him about the Lord. But it was after that, when they were in bed, that she made him feel like a man, even after he was crippled and had lost his manhood.

A tear came to Samuel's eye and ran down the deep creases of his face. Laying aside the cedar and the knife, he wiped his eyes and head with the bandana. He took his pipe and tobacco pouch from his overalls. He packed the brown leaves into the corncob bowl. He swiped a kitchen match across the bench. He took several long puffs to draw the flame into the dry tobacco. In the still air, smoke hovered above his head. He enjoyed the pipe and a few moments of quiet thought.

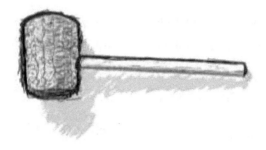

For Samuel, Rachel was the finest woman ever. She had made him a better man in many ways. She had taught him to hold his temper, to be more considerate, to appreciate life even when it was hard, and it was hard. Most of all, Rachel had taught him to pray, not trying to use fancy language, but just to speak to the Lord as an elder friend.

Ever since Rachel had passed, Samuel thought about her every day. He wondered if he could live without her at first. For a time he wondered if he even wanted to. Sorrow, he learned, flows like the tide, rising and then ebbing away.

After John Howard died less than a year ago, Samuel noticed that whenever he thought of Rachel, Maggie soon came to his mind. Mostly he felt sad for the widow and her loss. He just wanted to comfort the fine woman who lived across the sandy track. Recently, he felt differently. Maggie had surprised him with the way she had taken care of herself and Sally. Maggie was a strong woman like Rachel. And she was a handsome woman too. Samuel realized that now there were times when he thought of Maggie without Rachel even coming to mind.

He finished his pipe, knocked out the ashes into the sand, and ground them with his boot. He put the pipe and tobacco in his pocket and returned to his whittling.

As the cedar block slowly took the shape of a woman, Samuel gently carved smooth hips and rounded bosoms. It had been a long time since Samuel had moved his hands over the curves of a woman. The wooden doll was a poor substitute.

Sally was no kin to Samuel. She was a neighbor, the daughter of John and Maggie Howard. The Howard family lived across the sandy track that followed the river. Sally was old enough to be a grown-up woman, but she would always be a child.

Maggie had the fever when she was ripe with the baby. When she gave birth, the little girl came out backwards.

Some said that John might not be Sally's daddy. Both John and Maggie were as black as swamp water, black like Samuel, the way Gullah folks are supposed to be. But Sally was born nearly white.

Some said the foreman at the lumber mill made John a wagon driver, sending him all over the county to load logs. It was like King David putting Bathsheba's husband, Uriah, on the front battle line to get him out of the way.

While John was gone, some say the foreman, a conniving little short white man, had his way with Maggie, just like King David had his way with Bathsheba. He took another man's wife for his own. It was not because Maggie wanted anything to do with the foreman, but because he threatened to hurt John if Maggie didn't give in to him. Rachel thought Maggie might have submitted in the flesh to protect her husband. But, Rachel knew Maggie would never willingly submit to any man she didn't love in her spirit.

Once Maggie was with child, the foreman put John back to running the saw. Some say the white foreman took up with another Gullah woman.

Samuel knew the foreman. He was a bossy little white man, and his soul was as dark as a water moccasin.

Sally wasn't right from the start. The preacher said she had an evil spirit that addled her. Samuel said, "Evuhbody a child of Gawd."

It wasn't just that her color was different. It was her mind, too. As she grew, she took on a darker color, like walnut lumber. Even though her color got better, her mind didn't. It got worse. Still, John and Maggie loved their child, blaming whatever was wrong on the fever. They never talked about the foreman. But they both knew, and Samuel knew, too. Samuel said, "Gawd loves evuhbody, even dem dat don't know hit."

Samuel looked at the cedar figure. The carving was nearly finished. Maggie could make clothes for the doll, and Sally would have her Christmas present. After a few more strokes with his knife, Samuel folded the sharp blade and put the knife in his pocket. He picked up a handful of sand and ground the carving in his calloused fist using the sand to smooth all of the knife marks out of the grain. He blew the grit and dust from the figure and wiped it clean with his shirttail.

Using the cedar walking stick, Samuel stood up. He had been a tall man before the accident at the lumber mill. Above the waist, he still carried himself well. His chest and shoulders were powerful, but his left leg was crippled and weak. He kept his full white beard neatly trimmed. Beneath white eyebrows, his eyes were black and usually gentle, filled with kindness, though he was capable of rage. His heart was both courageous and tender. His mind was filled with the wisdom of his years.

Samuel wiped his brow with the bandana and put the felt hat back on his head. He put the doll in the ample pocket of his overalls and hobbled toward the house. Climbing the log steps was awkward. He had to step up with his good right leg and then drag his left leg up to the step, balancing with the walking stick. He climbed seven steps, one at a time. Once on the porch, he walked through the blue-framed door.

The house was little more than a shanty, a one-room wooden structure with a tin roof. One side the room had a bed, a ladder-back chair, and a dresser. Above the dresser was a cracked mirror.

The opposite side of the house featured a wood-burning stove, a table, and overturned nail kegs that served as stools. A galvanized tub and a five-gallon galvanized bucket completed the furnishings.

Inside, Samuel could smell the inviting aroma of black-eyed peas simmering in an iron pot on the woodstove. The peas flavored with a hambone were his supper. In fact, Samuel had peas or beans, rice or grits, for almost every meal. If there was meat in the pot, it was special. Eli Solomon gave him some salted pork every month. That didn't last very long because Samuel shared with Maggie and some of his other neighbors. The hambone in the pot tonight was different. Samuel stole it from his boss, Richard Meade.

Chapter Four

Professor Rosen:

The United States Lighthouse Service published *The Pink Book,* precisely entitled *Instructions to Light-Keepers and Masters of Light-Vessels, 1902.* This one-hundred-six-page manual was issued to each lighthouse keeper. It detailed all the duties and responsibilities of the job. Some were obvious, like understanding the beacon apparatus and cleaning and lubricating the clockwork mechanism. Other interesting details from this book included regulations about the colors of paint to be used on every building and feature of government property, how to store and transport the oil used as fuel, the exact recording of expenditures and a daily log, and even a prohibition against cutting any tree on the property. As a loyal lighthouse keeper, Eli Solomon ordered his life in strict compliance with *The Pink Book.* As a devout Jew, he lived by the higher authority of the Torah. Sometimes the two contradicted each other.

Sunday, December 17, 1916

Following morning prayers and the daily routine of extinguishing the twin wicks of the lamp in the lighthouse, Eli descended the stairs and whistled for the dog. Inside the keeper's house, Eli removed his boots, his hat, and his coat. He melted goat butter in a cast-iron frying pan and cracked the four guinea eggs into the hot oil. He stirred and scrambled the eggs until done. Dividing the eggs between his own plate and the dog's dish, he sat at the table, blessed the food, and thought about the week ahead.

Officer Roy Holden, the inspector for the United States Lighthouse Service, was due to visit the Georgetown Light before the end of December. In previous years, the fourth-quarter inspection had come after December 25.

Since arriving in South Carolina, Eli had learned that many Christians in America, much like Christians in the Ukraine, arrange their lives around the day called Christmas. He was sure that Inspector Holden would plan his visit sometime during the last week of the year. Eli wanted to be ready. Officer Holden made a point of surprising Eli by making his visits unannounced. It seemed that the inspector was intent on catching the lighthouse keeper in violation of one regulation or another.

On this bright, warm Sunday morning, Eli scattered corn for the guineas, turned the Nubians out to graze on the dunes, inspected his garden, and completed all of his other morning chores. He updated his logbook just before eating a light noon meal.

In the afternoon, Eli did his own inspection of the light station. Using a pencil stub, he jotted notes on a pocket pad, listing things that needed attention. He included places that needed touching up with paint or required minor repairs. At the top of the page, he wrote, *paint the skiff*.

When his inspection was completed, Eli climbed the stone steps of the tower. Circling the deck surrounding the lantern room, he removed a dead gull. Attracted by the bright beam, the bird had crashed into the tower. He swept the lantern room and down the tower stairs, stopping along the way to clean cobwebs and dust from the staircase windows and recesses.

Eli's duties included cleaning the grounds. He walked the perimeter of the triangular property carrying a burlap bag for trash and a sharp stick to pick up debris. Along the woods, he gathered several dead pine limbs that would become kindling for his stove. He piled them near the garden. A red-wing blackbird flew to a perch in a cedar tree. Eli saw deer scat nearby but no evidence of damage to the vegetables and herbs from animals. Everything on North Island needed rain. Eli could not afford to spare cistern water for the parched plants. He did use the leftover wash water on his garden, a practice he learned from his grandmother.

On a loblolly pine near the edge of the forest, Eli saw the telltale scratches left by a black bear searching for grubs. In December, on North Island, female black bears were usually hibernating with newborn cubs. The males continued to roam the forest, especially in warm weather. Judging from the height of the claw marks on the tree, the bear was large. The bark was peeled from the tree higher up than Eli could stretch.

The lighthouse keeper took his time strolling along the ocean side of the government tract. The Atlantic was eerily calm as it had been for most of the month. Except for scattered driftwood and a few interesting shells, there was almost no litter to collect along the ocean shore. He did pick up a nearly perfect lettered olive shell that was rolling in the surf. Eli put the specimen in the pocket of his shirt. It would be a beautiful addition to the collection on the windowsill. He continued walking with his dog, enjoying a pleasant Sunday afternoon.

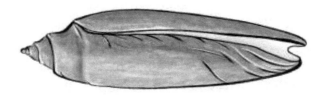

Eli sat down in the warm sand, pausing to soak up the beauty of North Island. He put his head back, resting it in the crook of his arm. In June, it was near this spot on the beach that he had found the distinct tracks of a female loggerhead turtle. She had come ashore to lay her eggs near the dunes. He had also seen the prints of a marauding raccoon that had raided the turtle nest to feast on the eggs.

Eli gazed into the late afternoon sky. There were no clouds. A faint crescent of the waning moon was set in the blue canopy. A formation of pelicans glided overhead, casting fleeting shadows on the sand. Melchizedek stretched out next to him. Eli scratched the dog's ears, and the animal leaned in to his touch. Both enjoyed moments like this.

The ridicule of Richard Meade was thirteen miles away. The harangue of Inspector Roy Holden was infrequent. The fire of Odessa was half a world and twenty years removed. But the sorrow in his heart for the loss of his wife and daughter was with him every day.

Richard Meade was a boisterous, abrasive man who owned and operated a small general store on the far end of Front Street, Meade's General Store. Among the residents of Georgetown, Richard Meade stood out as an irascible bigot. His objection to Jews was equal to his contempt for Blacks. The storekeeper despised the lighthouse keeper though the Lighthouse Service had a contract with his business. Meade treated the one man who helped him most, Samuel Pringle, with unrelenting ridicule. Eli thought it odd that a man could hold so much hatred for the people he depended on for his livelihood. But then, Meade was suspicious and resentful of anyone different from himself.

Richard Meade had questioned Eli about his work. "What does a Jew find to do out there on that island all by himself? Besides lighting the flame in that tower, what else is there to do? You must have the most boring life of anybody in Georgetown County."

The life of a lighthouse keeper was solitary, but it was certainly not boring. There was always plenty of work to do. *The Pink Book* of the Lighthouse Service dictated an exacting schedule. Keeping a detailed log was required. But moments like these made it all worthwhile. Eli cherished the time he had to see the ongoing drama of North Island play out. The natural interaction between loggerhead turtles and raccoons was just one example.

Solitude is not the same as loneliness. For Eli, his solitary life on North Island had been a balm for his soul. He still grieved for his wife and their daughter. But they were gone. He had Melchizedek, and his work, and North Island.

His life on North Island was satisfying. His work as a lighthouse keeper gave him a sense of purpose. Each day presented the opportunity for prayer and contemplation.

As surely as the female loggerheads needed the sandy dunes above the high tide line to lay their eggs and the raccoons needed a source of food for their scrounging ways, Eli and his dog, the goats and the guineas, the red wolves and the black bears had all found their place on North Island. It was a good place to call home.

Suddenly, something ran out of the woods to his left. Both Eli and the dog sat up. Neither made a sound. A large whitetail buck loped from the yaupon scrubs on the dunes and plunged into the surf. The deer swam out to the breakers. Only his head, crowned with a huge rack of antlers, showed above the blue-green water. The big buck emerged from the waves as quickly as he had entered, disappearing over the dunes further up the island.

My life is anything but boring.

Eli turned his gaze back to the ocean. A large mullet jumped, fleeing something beneath the surface. One pelican peeled away from a passing formation in pursuit of the fish. In the curl of the low waves, Eli saw a school of bluefish moving south. He and Melchizedek could look forward to catching a bluefish supper as a Hanukkah delicacy.

Rising to his feet, he continued combing the beach. "Solitary but not alone," he said to the dog in Yiddish.

As the afternoon wore on, Eli rounded the tip of North Island at the jetty. A large live oak had been uprooted and stranded on the point by a hurricane in July. Eli had been gleaning firewood from the tree since August. He made his way around the obstruction and followed the shoreline.

Eli continued patrolling the beach around the point where the shore left the Atlantic and followed the edge of Winyah Bay. He gazed out across the big water of the bay. She was a fickle and capricious lady, sometimes tempestuous, but now as calm as could be. The low tide uncovered trash. Glass bottles and tin cans, jettisoned by fishermen and boaters, littered the sand.

Humans are foul creatures, he thought.

Eli retrieved each piece of debris, including bits of wet newspaper. If the print was still legible, he read what he could make out. Along with an occasional coin, the discarded newspapers were his favorite finds.

In this Sunday's collection, he found a full front section of the *New York Times*. Eli carefully opened the damp pages and scanned the headlines. He learned that Allied forces had turned back the Germans in the Battle of Verdun. He read that Bulgaria had declared war on Romania and that Italy had declared war on Germany.

At his feet, in the shallow surf, he spotted a large cockle shell. He picked it up to admire the shape and the color of the find. Brown markings on the ridges of the outside contrasted beautifully with the smooth pink interior of the shell. The fine specimen would find a place on his windowsill.

A soggy fragment of the *New York Times* sports section revealed that Grover Cleveland Alexander had pitched his sixteenth shutout of the season.

Another scrap from an unidentified newspaper reported that a great white shark had killed four people and injured another off the New Jersey shore. He looked up from his beachcombing, out toward the jetty and the breakers beyond.

There are creatures beyond the imagination out there in that vast sea. The Leviathan from the wisdom of Job and the fish that swallowed Jonah were only two of many.

As he stooped to pick up a broken whiskey bottle, Eli saw a piece of cloth protruding from the muddy sand of Winyah Bay, a garment of some sort. With the stick, Eli lifted the unusual find from the mire. He was astounded at the discovery. It was a woman's undergarment, a muddy corset.

Eli stared in amazement. Though he recognized what the muddy, lacey garment was, he hadn't seen one in a very long time. He quickly deposited the corset in the burlap bag with the other trash.

His imagination took over. What had happened on this beach and when? Where was the lady who wore the corset? Judging by the ample size of the item, she would certainly have been noticed without it. He tried to block the possibilities from his mind, but he could not.

Looking across the empty water, Eli wondered if there had been a boating accident. Maybe the lady was a drowning victim. The scenarios were almost limitless and ranged from the risqué to the tragic.

How would he dispose of this unseemly find? And then, Eli raised the most disturbing question of all. What if Officer Roy Holden somehow found the corset?

Eli went back to the task of collecting rubbish from the beach along the bay. The low tide might reveal other surprises. He went to the government property line and a little beyond before he crossed the dunes to put the burlap bag and the trash stick away in the storeroom. For now, he would leave the corset in the trash sack. He would get rid of it all later.

The Lighthouse Service regulations required regular maintenance of every building and every piece of equipment on the government property. Special care was demanded for the oil shed because kerosene fumes were highly flammable. Eli checked the fuel shed one last time. Everything was in order. As he locked the shed, he looked up at the towering loblolly pine tree.

It is too close to this oil shed, he thought.

Back in the house, Eli placed the lettered olive and the large cockle on the windowsill with the other shells in his growing collection. Then, he decided what to have for supper. It would be bread and cheese again. But first, Eli had to attend to his most important task of the day.

He collected the cloth bag from the peg near the door and a box of matches issued by the Lighthouse Service. Regulations required that only official matches be used.

Guineas scurried around him and began seeking out their roost in the trees. Eli whistled loudly, and the big dog herded the Nubians into their sturdy pen. Eli had built the pen from driftwood, much of it from a shipwreck further up the island. A storm three winters earlier had uncovered the aging remains. Eli had laboriously hauled each piece of wood down the beach to construct the goat enclosure and the guinea coop.

The lighthouse keeper climbed the stairs to the top of the tower. An osprey left the tall pine tree near the oil shed, winging its way toward the setting sun across Winyah Bay. From the cloth bag, Eli removed the yarmulke, placing it on his head instead of the Lighthouse Service cap. As was customary, he did not use the prayer shawl for evening prayer. The lantern room again became a sanctuary as he gently swayed and recited:

Praised are You, Lord, our God, Ruler of the Universe
Whose word brings on the dusk of evening.
Your wisdom opens the gates of dawn:
Your understanding regulates time and seasons.
The stars above follow their appointed rounds, in response to Your divine will.
You create day and night.
You alternate darkness and light.
You remove the day and bring on the night;
You separate one from the other.
The Lord of Hosts is Your name.
You are our living God:
May You rule over us as You rule over nature:
Praised are You, O Lord, who brings the evening dusk. Amen.

Eli prayed in Hebrew, but it was mostly by rote. He knew the language of the Ukraine, but, like many Jews of Eastern Europe, he spoke Yiddish most of the time. He knew Hebrew well enough to pray with other Jews who spoke the language of the Torah comfortably. He was even able to read in the Hebrew language. But he had difficulty understanding the language of Zion, something he deeply regretted. His memorized prayers were in Hebrew. His spontaneous prayers were in Yiddish.

His prayer ended, Eli struck an official match and lit the double-wicked lamp. After he released the weight that rotated the Fresnel lens, the steady beam of the North Island Light circled across the Atlantic Ocean and swept the shores of Winyah Bay all the way to Georgetown. The sun disappeared beyond the water and the trees to the west, leaving traces of pink gradually fading to deep purple.

Between the intervals of the sweeping light from the beacon, Eli could see the stars filling the night sky. North Island was a place of sand and stars, like Hebron of old, where Abraham was given the covenant promise.

This place, thought Eli, *is holy ground.*

And then following a moment of reverence came a slightly irreverent thought.

In this hot, dry December, I certainly hope there will be no burning bushes.

On Sunday night, Eli drifted off to sleep in his hammock, wondering where the corset he had found on the shore had come from. Pondering the possibilities gave way to fantasies about a mystery woman, but his imagination soon turned to guilt. The devout Jew diverted his thoughts to his long-deceased wife, thinking of her instead of a strange woman without her clothing.

Eli remembered his wedding night, his eagerness, her timidity, his awkwardness, her willing submission. He recalled her sweet voice, her soft skin, her trusting eyes, and her innocent beauty. With memories of his wife in his head, Eli entered blissful sleep.

Chapter Five

Professor Rosen:

It happens very rarely, but sometimes an infant is born with a membrane covering the newborn's face. Such a child is said to be a caulbearer. The caul is a portion of the amniotic sac still clinging to an infant at birth. Because the caul covers the infant's face, the child is said to be born behind the veil.

Being born with a caul is not dangerous. The infant continues to receive oxygen and nutrition through the umbilical cord. At birth, the caul can quickly be cleared away from the baby's nose and mouth so that he or she can breathe. Among the slaves of All Saints Parish, a midwife would take special measures to preserve or to destroy the caul, depending on the wishes of the mother.

According to the research conducted by Genevieve Wilcox Chandler for the Federal Writer's Project in the 1930s, in Georgetown County, as in many other coastal areas around the world, it was widely believed that a child born with a caul could not drown. Fishermen and sailors especially prized a preserved caul. Sometimes a dried caul, called a mermaid's purse, would be sold to a seafarer as protection from drowning.

In the slave community, as in many other cultures, a caulbearer was destined to be a leader. A child born behind the veil was believed to be blessed with the gift of unusual insight and wisdom. The Buddha was said to be such a child. This is why Tibetan Buddhist monks often seek out a young caulbearer to become the successor to the Dalai Lama.

For the slaves of All Saints Parish, Moses was the supreme example of a caulbearer. The Bible speaks of Moses as having a veil over his face. As an infant, Moses was floated in a basket in the Nile River. As an adult, he led the Hebrew people safely through the waters of the Red Sea. He was a born leader, guiding people from slavery to the Promised Land. Moses spoke to God face-to-face, as one speaks to a friend.

Samuel Pringle was a caulbearer.

Sunday, December 17, 1916, continued

Fourteen miles away, on the bank of the Sampit River, Samuel Pringle packed tobacco into his pipe. He struck a match. Holding the flame above the corncob bowl, he drew the fire downward, lighting the shredded brown tobacco leaves. He tossed the match into the river. Exhaling smoke into the December night, he saw the sweep of the light from North Island.

Mr. Eli's on the job, he thought.

Though they saw each other only about once a month, Samuel knew the lighthouse keeper well. He was different because he was from someplace far away. But really, so was everybody, different and from someplace else. Even the ones that didn't think so, like old man Meade, who acted like he had been in Georgetown nearly since Noah landed the ark. Even Mr. Meade was from someplace else, and he sure was different.

On Saturday a week ago, Richard Meade's daughter had left on the Clyde Line steamer for New York City. It was a two-week trip, and she was due back two days before Christmas. Mr. Meade was on edge, worried about his only child way off up in the north. Miz Meade was fretting, too, according to Mr. Meade. Samuel had tried to give his boss man a wide berth. For Samuel this week before Christmas was sure to be like tiptoeing through a snake pit, and with his crippled leg and hip, Samuel was none too good at tiptoeing.

Samuel smoked and gazed at the night sky. The light of stars and the shrinking crescent moon shone in the dark night, unbroken by clouds.

T'ain't natural, dis warm dry December. Bound to be a storm 'fo long. Gotta be to break de spell.

Some said it was the last days, but Samuel had seen weather like this before.

Ain't nothin' much dat las' fo'eber.

Then, looking up again, *De Good Book say dat eben de sun, moon, and stars'll all pass away, and heaben and eart', too.*

Samuel Pringle had seen many changes in his lifetime. The midwife, who delivered Samuel into slavery, wanted to destroy the caul over his face. She wanted to make a tea from the membrane immediately, but Samuel's mother would have none of it.

"My baby has de gift. Don't rob dat from him."

Most of the All Saints slaves believed that Samuel had the gift of unusual insight, a way of understanding people that others didn't have. Some called it second sight. Samuel called it paying attention.

The slave community also believed that a child born with the caul could not die by drowning. So, from an early age, Samuel was put on the water. As a boy he swam with the porpoises in Winyah Bay. He learned to row. He had saved three people from drowning in the big hurricane that destroyed most of the rice.

As a young lad, he had been a taster and tender on the Alston family's rice plantations. The job required tasting the water and tending the floodgates. When the tide was going out, the water flowing down the rivers would be fresh, and the gates had to be open to allow the rice fields to flood.

But salt water kills the rice plants. When the tide was coming in, the water would taste salty, and the floodgates had to be closed.

After emancipation and the war's end, there was rioting and looting on some plantations. Samuel stayed right on working at Greenfield on the Black River. He then worked on shares for Miz Patience Pringle at Chicora Wood up along the Pee Dee, always on the water as a taster and a tender or just rowing folks from one place to another.

After the hurricanes flooded the fields with seawater and destroyed all of the rice, Miz Patience held out as long as she could, longer than all of the other planters. Most had sold out, many to Mr. Bernard Baruch, who bought up all of the plantations where the Waccamaw flowed into Winyah Bay. Miz Pringle still lived at Chicora Wood.

Lawd knows how long she might stay.

Samuel struck a match to relight his pipe. He took several long draws, exhaling the smoke in a cloud around his face. In the distance, the lighthouse circled its beam every fifteen seconds, the guardian of the night.

Mr. Eli's one of de most 'portant men in Georgetown. Some white folks oughta' treat him better.

Georgetown was a different kind of town than some. Most people Samuel knew were not so mean as folks he had heard about in other places. Most people in Georgetown got along good with each other, especially with the Jews.

Mr. Baruch, even though he called South Carolina home, was part of the second Yankee invasion, when folks from way up in the North came down to the South to buy land after the rice crops failed. They came in flocks like bobolinks, or rice birds. They bought the same land their daddies had tried to burn up during the war in the first Yankee invasion.

Mr. Baruch was somehow kin to Mr. Heiman Kaminski. Most folks knew Mr. Kaminski was head of the Georgetown Jews. Mr. Kaminski was pretty much the head of Georgetown.

Some folks said that Mr. Kaminski had pulled himself up by his own bootstraps. They said that after the war, Mr. Kaminski came to Georgetown from fighting for the Confederates. He had only two dollars to his name, and he started his own business.

Most folks knew that Mr. Kaminski owned half of Georgetown and had a lot to say about the other half. By now, he owned Kaminski Hardware, Willow Bank Boat Company, Pee Dee Steamboat Company, and the Medical Dispensary. He was Vice-President of the Bank of Georgetown, a director of the Georgetown Rice Milling Company, and an agent for the Clyde Line. Samuel trusted Mr. Kaminski. He was a good man, smart, too.

Mr. Kaminski even owned a tall ship named for his mama. The *Linah Kaminski* was a three-masted schooner that hauled lumber and cotton out of Georgetown and came back loaded with merchandise for the hardware store and fertilizer to sell to the farmers. Samuel had seen the big ship taking on cargo at the lumber mill on Saturday.

Some folks said Mr. Baruch bought 17,000 acres by himself, most all of Waccamaw Neck, to remake the Hobcaw Barony. Miz Patience Pringle had held on to Chicora after the storm of 1906 washed away the rice plantations forever.

Most people in Georgetown just wanted folks to get along, whites, Blacks, Jews, and everybody. Samuel heard some folks talk about a fellow by the name of Pitchfork Ben Tillman, a mean man who hated anybody different from himself. Some folks said he had stirred up a lot of trouble, but not in Georgetown.

Some folks said that meanness was strong up in Williamsburg County. Samuel had heard tell that white men covered up in white robes and hoods had lynched Black folks and burned Black families out as far away as Marion. Some said they even burned the cross of Jesus. That kind of meanness never got much of a foothold in Georgetown County.

There were still a few white people who hated Black folks and Jews. Mr. Eli had suffered stinging insults, especially from Richard Meade. Samuel had surely felt it, too, every single day except on Sunday when he didn't usually go into town.

Som'tin' done anger'd ole man Meade's blood, Samuel thought.

And then there was the foreman at the mill. He hated Black men but had a fondness for Black women. In the end, it might have caught up with him. He died when a logging chain broke, and a whole load of fresh-cut pine logs crushed the life out of him. Some folks said it weren't no accident.

The death of John Howard just last February might have been payback. Samuel knew John really good. It just wasn't like John to be careless. For him to stumble into a band saw and get his head just about cut off didn't sound like something John would do. Some said the foreman's cousin pushed him.

Samuel had taken it as his duty to look after Maggie and Sally the best he could. He felt sorry for Maggie, all alone as she was, taking care of her child, a little girl in a grown woman's body. Samuel had considered taking them in. It would be easier for all of them if they were like a family. Samuel's place was too small, smaller than Maggie's house. Besides that, the bigger problem was that Maggie was a good-looking woman years younger than Samuel. She needed a husband, and Samuel couldn't be a husband to her. He wanted to, all right. But his manhood was gone. He had all of the wanting, but he couldn't do anything about it. It wouldn't be fair to Maggie. Besides he was a fool to think she might even want to take up with an old man.

Now in the darkness of Sunday night, a mockingbird sang a medley from the top of a live oak. The water of the incoming tide lapped at the side of Samuel's old rowboat that was tied to his cypress log dock. Marsh grass on the bank of the Sampit barely rustled. The air was too still; the days too hot for December.

Da li'l Lawd Jesus wouldn't need no swaddlin' in dis heat. 't ain't natural, dis warm dry Christmas. Bound to be a storm 'fo long. Gotsta' be to a storm 'fo long.

Samuel finished his pipe, knocking the ashes into the soft pluff mud at the river's edge. He paused to gaze into the night sky and to relieve himself. Across the Sampit, in the fading light, an egret waded in the shallows. Through the fronds of a Palmetto tree, Samuel saw the waning moon, a fingernail moon Rachel had called it.

Then, turning with his cedar walking stick, he made his way back along the path of white sand, beneath the curtain of Spanish moss, toward his shanty.

He climbed the log steps to his blue-framed door, lifting his right leg and dragging his left. Inside, he sat in a ladder-back chair to take off his worn boots and socks. Standing without the walking stick, he took off his overalls and his shirt, tossing them on the chair. He lay down to sleep, using both hands to pull his left leg into the bed.

The next morning he would be with Old Man Meade at the store. Tonight he must rest. Under the covers, he calmed himself before he prayed aloud.

> Lawd, 'twas oonuh who woke me up dis mornin'.
> 'tis oonuh, dear Lawd, who can hep me sleep in peace.
> T'ank you fo' my many blessing,
> and please, dear Lawd, forgibe my many sins.
> If it be oonuh will, kindly wake me up again tomorrow mornin'.
> An', dear Lawd, please
> bring Mr. Meade's daughter home again safe and sound.
> Jesus' name, Amen.

Samuel slept. He dreamed of Rachel, and he dreamed of Maggie Howard.

Chapter Six

Professor Rosen:

My academic specialty is Judaism in Eastern Europe. I have a particular interest in Judaism in the Ukraine. Permit me to give you a little background that may help you understand why Eli Solomon came to Georgetown from Odessa.

In the 1890s, the Ukrainian city of Odessa was the fourth largest city in the Russian Empire after St. Petersburg, Moscow, and Warsaw. It was second only to Warsaw in Jewish population. By 1897, Jews were estimated to comprise 37 percent of the population. In 1890, Odessa exported 1,360,000 tons of grain, and by 1895, 2,000,000 tons were exported. By 1910, over 80 percent of the grain export companies in Odessa were owned by Jews

In addition to being heavily involved in grain exporting, Jews in Odessa were engaged in the retail trade. 56 percent of small shops were owned by the Jews, 63 percent of Odessa craftsmen were Jewish, and by 1900, 70 percent of Odessa banks were administered by the Jews. Jews were also heavily represented in the medical and pharmaceutical professions, 70 percent of the total in these professions being Jewish. 56 percent of the city's lawyers were Jews.

But anti-Jewish outbreaks were provoked by Russian and Ukrainian merchants and business people who viewed Jewish success with jealousy. They were later joined by the Russian government, which viewed such outbreaks as a safety valve against a revolutionary mood and anti-government feelings. This atmosphere became a strong stimulus to Odessa's Jews to emigrate to Palestine, Canada, the United States, and South America. For many years Odessa was known as a gateway to Zion.

Beginning in 1881, systematic persecution of Jews, called pogroms, swept through southern Russia. Mass Jewish defection resulted. 2 million Russian Jews emigrated from 1880 to 1920. In May 1882, a series of temporary laws by Czar Alexander III of Russia were put in place. The May Laws adopted a systematic policy of discrimination with the object of removing the Jews from their economic and public positions. This caused one-third of the Jews to leave, one-third to accept baptism, and one-third to starve.

In 1891, 20,000 Jews were expelled from Moscow. The Congress of the United States eased immigration restrictions for Jews from the Russian Empire. An estimated 393,000 Ukrainian Jews immigrated into the United States.

The Jews of Odessa were repeatedly subjected to severe persecution. Brutal pogroms were carried out in 1905. More than 300 Jews were murdered. Many Jews from Odessa fled abroad. One among those who left was Eli Solomon.

Monday, December 18, 1916

On Monday morning, two hours before dawn, Eli Solomon awoke in a cold sweat. The vivid memory of flames engulfing his home in Odessa was a persistent nightmare. He discovered the charred body of his wife in the ashes. His infant daughter was lost. Her remains were never found among the ashes of his home. Today would have been his little girl's birthday. Though twenty-one years had passed, the horror returned in his dreams, plaguing his soul and robbing him of peace. Sobbing in the dark, he prayed the lament of Psalm 6 in Hebrew.

Be merciful to me, Lord, for I am faint;
O Lord, heal me, for my bones are in agony.
My soul is in anguish
How long, O Lord, how long?
I am worn out from groaning:
All night long I flood my bed with weeping
And drench my pillow with tears.
My eyes grow weak with sorrow;
The Lord has heard my weeping.
The Lord accepts my prayer.

After a time, he rolled from the hammock to face the day.

After his usual visit to the pickle jar, Eli returned to the kitchen. He started a fire in the woodstove, brewed coffee, and prepared breakfast, again, a simple meal of bread and cheese. After blessing the food, he thought about the day ahead.

Once he had extinguished the light and completed the prescribed cleaning, he would need to turn his attention to a major project, maintenance of the skiff. In one week, he would make his monthly trip into Georgetown. The small boat needed a few minor repairs and a new coat of paint. The weather had been unusually hot and dry. The conditions were suitable for boat repairs, but the water level in the cistern was low. Eli also planned to take the goats to the freshwater pond up North Island so they could drink their fill. Though the Nubians did well in arid climates, they needed more water than the cistern could spare.

The day before him was full, but it was also a day of persistent remembrance. The pain of his deepest grief stayed with him throughout the day. It was the birthday of his daughter, Lenora. The nightmare that had awakened him reminded him of his daughter's birthday and the vivid horror of his home engulfed in flames. Eli had buried his wife according to tradition. The kind rabbi seemed to understand Eli's deep loss and had said words of remembrance for Lenora as well.

Eli cleaned the kitchen as he remembered his child's birth. On the last night of Hanukkah, 1895, Eli and his wife lit all eight candles in the menorah. A short time later, his wife went into labor. Eli summoned the midwife, and a few hours before dawn, Lenora lay in her mother's arms. Because she was born during Hanukkah, she was given the Hebrew name for light – Lenora. Today, had she lived, she would be twenty-one years old, a young woman. Eli recalled that he was twenty-one when Lenora was born.

Melchizedek barked from somewhere near the goat pen. Eli opened the door and peered into the morning darkness, listening to the dog bark as he patrolled the edge of the island forest. Something had threatened the goats, maybe red wolves, maybe a black bear, maybe a wild boar. Whatever the predator, nothing on the land was a match for Melchizedek. Predators in the water, though, were a different matter.

After tending to his feet and pulling on his boots, Eli picked up the cloth bag, left the porch, and walked to the lighthouse. The beacon circled the strong beam through a column of wood smoke rising above the house. The light fanned across the bay and back out over the Atlantic. Eli climbed the stone stairs to greet the morning. To the east first light was beginning to brighten the dark, star-filled sky. A waning moon hovered in the west above Winyah Bay and the four rivers beyond. Before snuffing the double wick, Eli waited for the sun to emerge from the ocean so that he could view the expanse of the sea in first light. The flat water reflected the sun's rays like a mirror. This December day would be like a day in September, warm and dry. But the ocean kept her secrets, and Eli knew many of them. Somewhere beyond this calm water, a storm was in the making.

Eli offered his morning prayers, adding a remembrance for Lenora.

The schedule of a lighthouse keeper was demanding and tedious with routine and repetitive work. Eli was required to keep an official log of his daily chores. Inspector Roy Holden checked the record each time he made his quarterly rounds. Eli's job required that he maintain the light and keep the lamp burning from sunset to sunrise. Every day he cleaned and polished the lens, checked and filled the oil lamp, and trimmed the wicks. He was also responsible for dusting and oiling the clockwork of the apparatus. The oil shed required special care because kerosene fumes were highly flammable. Lighthouse Service regulations required regular maintenance of every building and piece of equipment.

Station maintenance consumed the bulk of Eli's time. Still, he appreciated his job. The pay was meager, but he made more money in South Carolina than he could have ever earned in Odessa. Though the routine was demanding, it suited him just fine. Besides, Eli loved the sea, the solitude, and the wind.

Today, he must see to the skiff, the small boat vital to Eli's work. The craft was required to make the monthly trip to Georgetown, thirteen miles up the bay, to procure supplies. Eli timed the monthly voyage by the tides. Since the skiff was primarily a rowboat, going with the current saved time and energy, Eli's energy. On the incoming tide, it would take about five hours for Eli to row to Georgetown. While the tide was slack, he would buy supplies, always from Richard Meade, the disagreeable proprietor of Meade's General Store on Front Street. Though Mr. Kaminski's Mercantile was bigger and better, Meade had a contract with the Lighthouse Service.

Eli would have the skiff loaded and the cargo secured, as the tide turned. Once beyond the Sampit River and into the big water of

Winyah Bay, the outgoing tide made the trip back to North Island easier.

The skiff also served as a rescue boat. Though it was not intended for the open ocean, Eli had used it on two occasions to save lives.

A drunken sailor had tried to swim from his ship to the light. He said he had seen a pretty little blond girl running on the beach. Though a good swimmer when sober, the inebriated swab was caught in a riptide. Eli rowed well beyond the breakers to haul the man to shore. The sailor's ship picked him up two hours later from the lighthouse dock.

The previous fall, two teenage boys from Georgetown in a small boat were fishing for red drum near the jetties. The strong ebb tide carried the boat out through the channel into the open ocean. Eli took the skiff out and towed them back to the beach.

Though the Lighthouse Service issued the skiff, Eli had made several modifications to the small vessel, making it more efficient. In a matter of minutes, the rowboat could be converted into a sailboat. Eli added a mast fitted with a hand-sewn canvas sail. He fashioned a daggerboard that could be lowered into the water from the stern to serve as a keel. He attached a third oarlock to the transom that enabled him to use one oar as a rudder. If the winds were favorable, the skiff became a small sailboat somewhat like a smaller version of his grandpa's fishing boat on the Black Sea.

Eli examined the hull of the skiff where three days earlier, he had caulked along the seams between the boards. He sanded away the excess dried putty and applied a fresh coat of white paint. In the warm air, the paint would dry to the touch in a few hours. Then he could paint the interior of the skiff.

While he had the white paint at hand, he touched up a few places on the windowsills of the keeper's house and a few worn areas on the lighthouse that he could reach from the ground. His job complete, he cleaned the brush and returned the paint to the storage room.

He noticed the burlap bag containing trash and the corset he had found along the muddy shore of Winyah Bay. He needed to dispose of the trash, as was his routine, when he went into Georgetown.

His morning chores completed, Eli again ate bread and cheese for his noon meal. He scattered a fistful of corn for the bustling guineas. He whistled for the dog to gather the goats for the trip up North Island.

Eli was given his first two Nubians by Samuel Pringle. When he was newly assigned to the lighthouse, Eli was an assistant keeper to Ralph Goforth. When a vacancy occurred at the St. Augustine light in Florida, Goforth was reassigned to fill that position. It was then that Eli Solomon became the keeper of the North Island Light.

In those early days, Samuel Pringle rowed out to the inlet almost every Sunday, his only day off. Samuel fished in the channel and then tied up his bright blue rowboat at the lighthouse dock. He usually had fish to spare and would give Eli some of his catch. In turn, Eli gave Samuel as much salt pork as Samuel wanted. The pork was part of the regular ration distributed by the Lighthouse Service, but for Eli, it was not kosher, so he couldn't eat it.

Though the Jewish dietary laws were important to him, keeping kosher was something deeper for Eli. It was more than knowing what to eat and what to avoid. For Eli, it was an essential part of his spiritual path. Keeping kosher was far more than an obligation; it was a joyful obedience.

Roy Holden cut Eli's ration when he learned that he did not eat pork. Still, Eli had plenty to share with Samuel.

As the infrequent friendship developed between the Ukrainian immigrant and the former African slave, Samuel learned that Eli could enjoy fish, fowl, and mutton. It was Samuel who brought the first guinea eggs to the lighthouse keeper. Eli kept them warm until the keets hatched, giving him a start on his flock. The birds of African origin were well-suited to North Island.

Samuel also brought the first two goats, a buck and a doe, rowing them thirteen miles from Georgetown out to North Island. Samuel's only explanation was that he had found the eggs and the goats.

The Nubians were large, proud, and graceful dairy goats and, like the Guineas, were of African origin. The Nubians were all-purpose animals. Eli kept them for meat, milk, and leather. He had learned from his grandfather the kosher way of slaughtering and butchering an animal. He knew how to cook the meat so that it was tasty, as well as kosher. The Jewish lighthouse keeper planned to slaughter one of the kids, a young male, for Passover in the spring, unless, of course, he could find a lamb. So far, he had never seen a lamb on North Island.

Eli's Nubians produced more milk than was needed to nurse their kids. Since the Nubian breeding season was much longer than that of other breeds, Eli had high butterfat milk almost year-round. The kids were healthy and hearty, and, with their antics, they provided constant entertainment. The goats thrived on weeds and required little water. Nubians were the best dairy goat breed for hot weather. Like Eli, the Nubians were well suited to North Island. Still, they needed a deep drink of fresh water.

In the afternoon, Eli picked pennyroyal from his garden. Crushing the fragrant herb in his palms, he rubbed it on his forehead and neck and around his wrist and ankles to discourage biting insects. Most of the time, Eli did not bother with repelling insects, but a trip to the pond was the exception. Even in December, black gnats, pesky mosquitoes, and biting flies were a nuisance.

Eli lined a basket with pine straw. Though it was not the season for duck eggs, if the guineas were laying eggs out of season, the mallards might also be confused by the unusually warm weather.

At the goat pen, he gave a sharp whistle, and Melchizedek brought the goats in a single file to walk behind Eli. They followed a sandy path through the forest of cedars, yellow pines, and palmetto palms. Along the way, Eli noticed animal tracks in the sand. North Island was home to a rich variety of wildlife. Deer tracks were plentiful. He also saw another tree with the bark clawed away, marks probably made by the same large black bear that scarred the tree near the garden. The bear had been searching for grubs.

As they came into a clearing, Eli saw three turkey vultures circling overhead. The dog left the path, trotted through the undergrowth, and came to a stop. Leaving the goats in the clearing, Eli followed the dog.

The dog had found the remains of a fawn. The young deer had been torn apart, almost certainly by a pack of red wolves. The skeleton had been picked clean. Only a few rotting morsels remained for the buzzards circling above.

Eli and the dog rejoined the Nubians for the trip up the island. Eli thought about the site of the kill.

If wolves did that to a fawn, what would they do to a Nubian kid?

The column of man, goats, and dog trekked on toward the pond, Eli saw wild boar scat. There were no human footprints other than those made by Eli's boots.

As far as he knew, he was the only human inhabitant this far south on the island. Before the series of hurricanes that ravaged the area ten-to-twelve years earlier, several Black families were living in wooden huts along the bay side. The fierce storms destroyed the poorly constructed homes. Lives were lost, and the survivors abandoned the island. Eli had visited the former site of the small community, and there was nothing left.

Fishermen told stories about an old African roaming the island at night. He was said to have hair and beard as white as bleached sand, giving him a ghostly look. Eli had lived on North Island for seven years and had never seen even a trace of another resident. There was often evidence of visitors. For example, there was the puzzling discovery of a lady's corset half-buried in the mud of Winyah Bay at low tide. Eli knew he needed to get rid of the garment stashed in the burlap bag in the fuel shed.

There was also the persistent story of a little blond-headed girl. She was said to be the spirit of the daughter of a former keeper of the lighthouse. Her widowed father took her with him whenever he made the long trip to Georgetown. On a return trip to North Island, they encountered a sudden severe storm. The lighthouse keeper tied his daughter to his back as a precaution. When the small boat capsized, father and daughter were washed into the heaving waves of Winyah Bay. The lighthouse keeper swam with all of his might, but when he arrived exhausted on the beach near the lighthouse, in spite of his efforts, his little daughter had not survived.

Eli had heard the story several times. Samuel Pringle told him the little girl was a ghost. The former slave wanted Eli to paint the doorframe of the keeper's house bright blue, haint blue, he called it. Samuel said the blue color would keep spirits out of the house, even though the little girl seemed to be a helpful spirit.

Eli had explained to Samuel that the bright blue paint was unauthorized by *The Pink Book*, the Lighthouse Service, and by Officer Roy Holden.

Those who reported seeing the diminutive blond-headed ghost were enchanted, much like the drunken sailor had been, the one Eli rescued from the riptide. The tradition was that the little blond-headed girl appeared only at certain times, always to warn of an approaching storm. Two days after Eli saved the sailor, a tropical storm blasted North Island.

For Eli, the story of the little girl who died as her father carried her on his back brought to mind his own little Lenora. Eli had no chance to save her or to bury her. He could not find any trace of his child.

He paused as tears flooded his eyes.

Walking along the sandy path toward the pond, Eli tried to imagine how his daughter might have looked on this, her twenty-first birthday. Surely, she would have been as beautiful as her mother. Following the path leading further up the island, Eli shed more tears.

As they approached the blackwater pond, Eli slowed the pace. He wiped the tears from his eyes on the sleeve of his denim shirt.

Eli had used a length of rope to make a collar for each goat, and each collar was fitted with a heavy brass bell taken from an old horse harness. The bells served a double purpose. The constant ringing helped Eli and Melchizedek locate the goats. The bells also gave notice to wild animals to stay away. Even predators were a little wary when they heard five bells ringing in unison.

The only natural source of fresh water on North Island, the pond was reliable even when the cistern was low on water. But the pond was also home to a variety of insects, ducks, turtles, snakes, and two large alligators. As the pond came into view, Eli saw the pair of alligators sunning themselves on the opposite bank. Though alligators are usually docile, rarely eating, in the winter months, Eli was cautious. The unusually hot December weather might make the large reptiles unseasonably active. Warm sunshine would stir a cold-blooded body into activity.

He spoke softly to Melchizedek. The dog began searching the grass around the edges of the pond, stopping at intervals and holding very still. Eli moved forward and removed two wild duck eggs from a single nest his dog discovered. He was usually careful to leave more eggs than he gathered. Now there was no use. If young mallards hatched in December, they would not survive. The mallards that visited North Island laid their eggs in the spring. But the weather had been so warm, even the ducks were mixed up.

With two fresh eggs nestled safely in the basket of pine straw, Eli spoke softly to his dog again. Without a sound, Melchizedek nudged the Nubians one at a time toward the black water's edge. Once he had lined the goats up at the pond, the dog slipped into the dark water, positioning himself between the alligators and the goats.

As the goats drank deeply, Melchizedek paddled into deeper water. Eli watched. The two large reptiles stirred but remained on the bank. *Melchizedek certainly must have some water breed in his bloodline,* thought Eli. The dog, though protecting the goats, enjoyed the refreshing dip.

Then out of the corner of his eye, Eli saw a long black snake swimming toward his dog. The thick body and diamond-shaped head of the serpent left no doubt - a cottonmouth water moccasin. Still paddling in deeper water, Melchizedek had not seen the snake.

Eli gave a shrill whistle. He shouted loudly in Yiddish, warning his dog of the nearby danger. The goats scrambled back from the water. Melchizedek turned in the water to see the large viper no more than six feet from him.

Then, out of the depths of the black water came the large gaping jaws of another reptile, a monster alligator, his massive maw opened for the kill. Suddenly, the gigantic jaws slammed shut. The water churned as the alligator thrashed his head and tail from side to side. Then, the gigantic reptile went into a death roll.

Eli watched in amazement as the alligator turned the writhing water moccasin in his mouth, swallowing him headfirst in one gulp. The alligators on the opposite bank plunged into the pond. Melchizedek splashed ashore near Eli.

The dog shook the water from his coat and gave a defiant bark. The goats nervously fell into single file and headed down the sandy path away from the blackwater.

Eli made a mental note. *The pond is home to three, not two, large alligators.*

Eli took a long deep breath. He heart was beating fast. The words of Richard Meade ran through his head, "You must have a boring life out there on that island."

Life on North Island was anything but boring.

The procession of lighthouse keeper, Nubian goats, and Melchizedek returned to the south end of North Island. The sun was setting over Winyah Bay. The dog herded the goats into their pen. A few at a time, the Guinea fowl found their roost in the big live oak. With official Lighthouse Service matches in hand, Eli climbed the 124 steps to the top of the tower.

Before lighting the lamp in the tower, Eli offered his evening prayers from the lantern room. He and Melchizedek shared a duck egg and goat cheese omelet for supper. Eli again prayed, thanking God for protection. He remembered Lenora and his wife. His heart ached. More tears trickled down his cheeks, along the sideburns, and into his beard.

The day following her death, according to the custom of Jewish tradition, Eli's wife had been interred. He could hardly remember the service. The *Hevra Kaddishah*, the woman designated for the task, had prepared his wife's body for burial. The sympathetic rabbi who conducted the funeral recognized Eli's double loss. He said words intended to comfort, but there was no comfort. Eli's life was changed forever.

Though no one knew how the fire started, Eli knew in his heart of hearts that the fire had been deliberately set. He had been at a meeting in the synagogue, a meeting of Jewish leaders to pray for the cessation of the pogroms. When Eli left the synagogue, his house was in flames, his family was gone.

A familiar but unwelcome bitterness crept into his soul. He shouted aloud into the night the Hebrew lament, "My God, my God, why have you forsaken me?"

The dog came to his side.

Eli threw off his work clothes and fell into his hammock, sobbing softly. The dog drew closer.

The strong beam of the North Island Lighthouse circled overhead as Eli wept until sleep came.

Chapter Seven

Professor Rosen:

In his recent book, *The History of Georgetown County, South Carolina*, George C. Rogers gives a detailed account of Chicora Wood, a rice plantation on the Pee Dee River. In *Chronicles of Chicora Wood* and *A Woman Rice Planter*, Elizabeth Allston Pringle writes her memories of the history and daily life on the plantation.

The home, built before 1819 on 915 acres of land, was the residence of the second of two South Carolina governors from Georgetown, Robert Francis Withers Allston. Allston was born in 1801. He graduated from the United States Military Academy. After he served with the Army Engineers and after his father's death, he returned to Georgetown to help his mother operate and manage Chicora Wood.

Allston married Adele Petigru in 1832. They had ten children, five who lived to adulthood. At his death in 1864, near the end of the Civil War, this distinguished statesman owned seven plantations. He left one plantation and one hundred slaves to each of his five children. A sixth plantation was sold with the revenue divided equally among his wife and his children. Chicora Wood was also left to his widow.

In her history, *Georgetown Rice Plantations*, published in 1955, Alberta Morel Lachicotte summarizes the story of Elizabeth Allston Pringle. Elizabeth married John Julius Pringle soon after the Civil War. He lived only six more years. Elizabeth remained at Greenfield, the Pringle plantation, until the death of her mother. She then purchased her childhood home, Chicora Wood. Under her management, Chicora

Wood continued to produce Carolina Gold Rice until 1906. It was the last of the Georgetown plantations to produce rice. With Elizabeth Allston Pringle's death in 1921, Chicora Wood passed out of the Allston family.

In our story, Samuel Pringle was born a slave at Chicora Wood. He moved with Patience Pringle to Greenfield after the war and later moved back to Chicora Wood.

W. J. Cash in *The Mind of the South* wrote that after the Civil War, the pattern of Southern life did not change. Many slaves remained as laborers on the plantations working as sharecroppers for their former masters. As farms and factories replaced the plantations, former slaves and their offspring worked for the prosperous owners alongside impoverished whites.

In Georgetown, the glory days of Carolina Gold Rice plantations gave way to lumber manufacturing. Wealthy northern merchants owned the Atlantic Coast Lumber Company. After a disastrous fire in 1913, they rebuilt plant. It covered fifty-six acres in the bend of the Sampit River. The Company controlled timber rights on 250,000 acres in eight South Carolina counties. The economy of Georgetown was revived with lumber and by the sweat and blood of good people like Samuel Pringle.

Monday, December 18, 1916, continued.

Samuel Pringle had been on the water his whole life. From the day he was baptized in the shallows along the river's edge, he was always near the water.

"Oonuh was borned into dis world knowin' how to swim," his mama told him.

The other slaves at Greenfield called him L'il Water Bug. Traveling by a boat of one kind or another had been his regular transportation. As a young boy, he started out with a handmade *bateau* carved by his uncle from a cypress log. He poled or paddled the flat-bottom boat up and down the Black River. He had used the blue boat for more than twenty years from the time when he was a taster and tender at Chicora Wood.

Some folks said it was a lifeboat from a tall ship that had washed up in the pluff mud on Cat Island after a storm. It was found by a fisherman and towed into the harbor in Georgetown. Miz Pringle's foreman bought the boat for a dollar for use on the plantation.

Some said the boat was cursed because it had come from a ghost ship. Before he ever put it in the water, Samuel painted the boat blue, haint blue.

After the big hurricane ten years ago, when Miz Patience decided to quit growing rice, she gave the old rowboat to Samuel as a parting gift.

"You take it with you, Samuel. You've been rowing it now for ten years. Nobody else knows what to do with it anyway."

He repaired it time and again. He kept pine pitch on the deep v-shaped hull. He had replaced a couple of the ribs. He kept all four oarlocks well oiled, though he only used the ones aft. It came to him with only three oars. One was missing. He kept the third oar stowed beneath the starboard gunwale. He caulked the inside seams and painted the boat at least once every year, always haint blue.

Before daylight, Samuel untied his rowboat from the cypress log dock beyond his shanty on the Sampit River. The accident at the lumber mill had crippled him so severely that he could hardly walk. Now, in his seventh decade, he rowed to work six days a week. Richard Meade called him a black water rat.

Before the big ripsaw fired a pine log at him, breaking his left thigh, Samuel didn't mind walking from the Gullah Line along the Sampit into Georgetown. He had never felt so much pain all at once in his whole life. The hurt was so bad he passed out right there in the sawdust with the saw still running. John Howard heard him cry out even above the sound of the saw. John picked him up on his shoulder and carried him all the way to Rachel. Some folks said he nearly died lying there in his bed waiting for the leg to mend. He thought he would have passed on, too, if it hadn't been for Rachel taking care of him like she did.

Neighbors followed butterflies through the swamp and the marsh to find the white flowers of the sweating plant. They gathered the stems and leaves of the fuzzy daisies. Rachel dried them in the sun and made boneset tea for Samuel nearly every day. When his bones finally did heal, they grew back crooked, and Samuel could hardly walk at all. His manhood was gone. But he could still row his boat.

His strong arms pulled the long oars through the dark water. The boat glided past the lumber mill. Samuel was forever indebted to John Howard. They had worked together at the mill since the plantation shut down. The Atlantic Coast Lumber Corporation had saved the economy of Georgetown after the rice was gone.

The company had given both John and Samuel a job. But the company had also cost Samuel the use of his left leg and his manhood. It had cost John dearly. It had cost him his life. A memory of the band saw digging into John's neck flashed through Samuel's mind. He pushed it away with a vision of Maggie.

The sun was rising over Winyah Bay. In the early light, sliding turtles lined up on a half-submerged cypress log to begin soaking up the sun. The cooters, as the Gullah folk referred to the turtles, predicted another hot December day.

Samuel tied the rowboat to the wharf behind Meade's General Store. He stood up in the boat, placed his walking stick up on the dock, turned, and sat on the rough boards, pulling his left leg up with both hands. He removed his sweat-stained hat and wiped his brow and head with the faded bandana. Using the stick, he hoisted himself upright. He leaned against a thick piling and took a leak into the water below. The backdoor of the store was open. Samuel walked in.

"Where in the hell have you been, you lazy nigga'?" asked Richard Meade.

"Good mornin', Mr. Meade." Samuel removed his hat, hanging it on a twenty-penny nail at the backdoor.

"Hopes oonuh and Miz Meade had a pleasant Sunday."

"Pleasant, hell. She's worried sick about our daughter. The girl wanted to go to New York, so we let her go. We haven't heard one damn word from her. Not even a postcard. She's supposed to be here on the *Cherokee* on Friday. Her life is in the hands of that Jew, Kaminski."

"I 'magine she be jest fine."

"Dumb, nigga'. Whatta you know? Help me get these shelves stocked before paying customers start coming through the door."

"Yes, suh, Mr. Meade."

Richard Meade was a tall man with a pockmarked face. Thin black hair was combed from one large ear to the other in an attempt to conceal a balding head. Black bushy eyebrows met on the bridge of his nose. His eyes bulged like frog eyes, often darting from side to side as if he were about to catch a fly. When he wasn't speaking, his mouth was a tight straight line with thin lips, just Like a frog's mouth. Most of the time, he was croaking loudly, except with paying customers. Then he was artificially pleasant, nasty nice.

Samuel carried heavy burlap bags of coffee beans and potatoes from the storage room to the front of the store, lifting them to his right shoulder and bracing himself with his left hand against the counter. He carried boxes of canned goods under his right arm, again balancing with his left hand on the counter, which ran the length of the store. He finished his work stocking shelves before the first customer arrived.

Meade had instructed Samuel never to speak to a customer unless spoken to first. Then he was to say no more than "Yes, Sir" or "Yes, Ma'am."

"Nobody wants to hear that stupid nigga' Gullah talk outta you," Meade scolded.

Meade had also warned him never to look a customer in the eye. Then he added, "If I ever catch you looking a white lady in the eye, I'll kill you."

Samuel had looked Richard Meade in the eye, and he had seen the fear in his soul. It was that fear that made him so mean and hateful. Evil came into people in different ways. Sometimes a person just started out evil from the beginning. The foreman at the lumber mill was that way.

De debil always in him.

Sometimes a person's soul was just taken over by the devil. They gave the tempter so much opportunity without any resistance. Roy Holden was like that.

He spend too much time on da' dark side."

For Richard Meade, evil entered him through his fears.

Dat's da' most usual way.

Most of the day, Samuel worked, stocking and straightening, sweeping and dusting, toting and fetching, for Richard Meade. Samuel could see his boss's fear in every conversation, in every reaction.

Business was slow throughout the day. Meade complained, often cursing the weather, blaming the December heat for the shortage of Christmas shoppers.

In the mid-afternoon, Mr. William Doyle Morgan, former mayor of Georgetown, walked into the store. He purchased a box of Cuban cigars. Bowing and scraping, Richard Meade acted like the president had come for a visit.

The mayor was an important man, for sure. Under his leadership, Georgetown had added electricity, telephone service, sewer facilities, rail connections, some paved streets, and sidewalks. Mr. Morgan was the president alright, the president of The Bank of Georgetown. Mayor Morgan had been responsible for deepening Georgetown harbor and for constructing the jetties at the mouth of Winyah Bay. Because of Mayor Morgan, Georgetown had a new public school. The federal government built a Post Office and Customs House while Mayor Morgan was in office. He was certainly an important man.

The mayor had only one hand. He lost his left hand, just above the wrist, years back. He often wore an artificial hand, but after his wife died, he didn't use it all the time. Today his left arm hung at his side without the hand.

As he was leaving, Mr. Morgan spoke to Samuel. "Hello, Samuel. You having a good Monday?"

Samuel, looking down at his feet, replied, "Yes, suh."

"Samuel, do you smoke?"

"Yes, suh."

"What do you smoke?"

Samuel looked at Meade. "Answer the mayor's question, boy."

"Smokes a pipe, suh."

"I want you to try one of these cigars."

Opening the newly purchased box, Mr. Morgan offered a fine cigar to Samuel.

Again, he looked at Meade. "The mayor's trying to give you something, boy."

Samuel picked up one of the cigars.

The mayor spoke, "Save it for Christmas, a treat to celebrate the birth of Christ."

"Yes, suh. T'ank oonah, suh."

"Samuel, do you have a family?"

Again, he looked at Meade. With fury in his eyes, Meade said, "Speak, boy."

The mayor said, "Samuel, look up. Richard Meade can't tell you who to talk to."

"Yes, suh," Samuel said, lifting his head slightly.

"Do you have a family?"

"No, suh, not now. My mama died fo' I come of age. My wife died here a while back. No children. I grew up on de plantation. Der evuhbody counts kin to most evuhbody else. We all be kin to each other. All de older ladies we called aunt. All de older mens we called uncle. Had many cousins but one cousin by blood dat I knowed 'bout. Mebbe died in de big hurricane. I'm only one lef'. But I live down on de Gullah Line. We all pretty much family down dere."

"I know where the Gullah Line is, over on the other side of the river."

"Yes, suh." Samuel said, looking back at his feet.

"You'll be there on Christmas Day?

101

"Yes, suh if nothin' don't be done happen'."

"I may pay you a visit after Christmas Mass."

"Yes, suh."

The mayor reached out his right hand to Samuel. Tentatively, Samuel shook hands with Mayor William Doyle Morgan.

The mayor spoke to Meade, "Thank you for getting these cigars in for me."

After the mayor left, Meade spoke to Samuel. "Kin to everybody just like a pack of rats. I don't care what the mayor says or thinks, as long as you work for me, you're my nigga,' and you'll do what I say. You understand me?"

"Yes, suh."

"Besides that pompous son-of-a-bitch ain't nothing but the Pope's nigga'. His Irish family built that Catholic Church. What's her name? Saint Mary's, Mother of God. The damn fool shot off his left hand duck hunting. That's when he went to work keeping books for that Jew Kaminski. Imagine an Irish Catholic hooking up with a Prussian Jew. Well, he can just prance himself back up to that fancy house on Prince Street or hike on over to the Gullah Line. He was mayor for fifteen years and did all that work to make Georgetown better, and they gave him a damn sterling silver punch bowl. It's probably the only pot he's got to piss in."

Richard Meade and Samuel Pringle worked in silence until late afternoon. Samuel thought about how Meade was so nice to the mayor when he came in to buy the cigars and how mean he had turned after the mayor left. He knew Mr. Meade was worried about his daughter, but something more, something evil tormented his boss man.

Both Meade and Samuel were surprised when Mrs. Patience Pringle entered the store in the late afternoon. She was old, much older than Samuel remembered. She wore a long gray dress with an embroidered white collar. A wool shawl was draped over her shoulders. A black felt hat with a gamecock tail feather sat atop her white hair. Though she was an old woman, Mrs. Pringle was still a proper lady.

"Good afternoon, Samuel." She spoke to the Black man first. "I hope you are well."

"Yes, ma'am," Samuel said, looking at the floor.

"And, Mr. Meade, are you and Mrs. Meade in good health?" she added.

"Yes, Mrs. Pringle. How can I help you today?"

"I have come to town to purchase a wedding gift for my great-niece. She is to be married in Charleston on New Year's Eve. I bought a sterling silver rice spoon for her at the jewelry store next door. Every new bride needs a rice spoon. I'm sure you'll agree."

"Yes, indeed," replied Meade.

"Sadly," Mrs. Pringle continued, "I have no rice to give with the spoon. I would like to purchase a small bag of rice to complete the gift."

"Certainly," said Meade. "Boy, get the lady a pound of rice."

"Yes, suh." Samuel scooped rice from a large burlap bag into a brown paper bag. He weighed the rice on the scale. It was a little over a pound.

He started to close the bag when Meade scolded, "Don't skimp on the lady's rice, boy. Put a little extra in the bag."

Samuel did as he was told.

"How much do I owe you, Mr. Meade?"

"Fifteen cents, Mrs. Pringle. The price has gone way up since the plantations disappeared. This is fine Carolina Gold Rice."

Samuel wished he hadn't said that. He knew how badly Miz Pringle felt about closing down Chicora Wood.

"Yes, Mr. Meade. I am familiar with Carolina Gold." Mrs. Pringle took a nickel and a dime from her coin purse. "I am well aware of how much effort goes into growing rice. It's probably worth twice that amount. Where was this rice grown, Mr. Meade?"

Meade answered, "Louisiana, I think."

"Then, Mr. Meade, how can it be Carolina Gold?"

"That's just what we call it. That's what everybody wants."

"Then, in truth, it is not Carolina Gold rice. It is Carolina Gold in the pockets of those who sell it."

"Yes, ma'am, Mrs. Pringle. You are certainly correct."

Turning to leave the store, she asked, "Samuel, may I have a word with you?"

Samuel looked at Meade. "Go on, boy. Do whatever the lady asks."

Samuel walked to the door with Miz Pringle. Out on Front Street, she turned toward him. Samuel turned away, glancing down at his feet.

"Samuel, look at me."

He averted his eyes, looking over her shoulder. She had never been tall, but she seemed even shorter. Her hair was completely white, as white as carded cotton. He gathered a faint aroma of lavender from the lady.

"Samuel, look me in the eye."

She held his gaze and continued. "Samuel, these are difficult times. A wise man named William Shakespeare once wrote, 'The times are out of joint.' I know these are hard times for you, too."

"Yes, ma'am. Times be hard for evhbody. Times be always outta joint."

His dark eyes moved to her cloudy blue eyes. He could see her soul, pure and honest.

"Samuel, you are a good man. You always have been. May I give you a gift?" She pressed a coin into his calloused palm. "Do something special with this. And thank you. Thank you for everything you have done for me."

"Much obliged, Miz Pringle. T'ank 'a ma'am."

Their eyes stayed fixed for a moment, with the affection of life-long friends. They had known each other for more than seventy years, from the time Samuel was born at Greenfield and Miss Patience was a little girl. Samuel rowed the young bride and her new husband, Mr. Pringle, down the Black River to Georgetown to board a tall ship for their honeymoon trip. Miz Pringle had a wedding feast for Samuel and Rachel when they got married. Even after the war and emancipation, Samuel remained loyal to Miz Pringle.

It was as if all of those years were squeezed into this single moment, into this one last exchange.

"Goodbye, Samuel," she said, tears coming to her eyes.

"Goodbye, Miz Pringle," Samuel attempted to hold back his own tears, but one escaped.

She turned away, walking down Front Street to a waiting carriage. Samuel watched the lady to whom he had given so much of his life. Though she was a white woman and he was a Black man, though she had been his owner, and he was her servant, there was a bond of respect between them.

His eyes followed her until she was gone. They had grown old after he left Chicora. Samuel sensed that he would never see Patience Pringle again until heaven, whenever that might be. Then, tears came to his eyes, and he blotted them with his bandana.

He looked down. In his palm was a five-dollar gold piece.

Back in the store, Richard Meade shouted at Samuel, "Nigga'. I warned you just today not to ever look a white woman in the eye. I saw you looking at her."

Meade was furious. He grabbed an ax handle out of a nail keg at the end of the counter and took a step toward Samuel. He had the look of a gigged bullfrog, eyes bulging out beneath a single knitted eyebrow.

He screamed at the Black man, "Boy, I'm gonna' teach you a lesson."

Meade swung the wooden oak handle toward the Black man's head. Samuel did not move back. He stared straight into the white man's protruding eyes, catching the ax handle in his strong left hand.

Meade desperately struggled with both hands to pull the smooth wood away, but Samuel twisted his left wrist, wrestling the handle from Meade's hands. He swapped the oak handle to his right hand, still fixing his gaze on Meade.

Meade's eyes were darting back and forth, filled with terror. Drops of sweat rolled down his forehead into his single bushy eyebrow.

Samuel dropped the handle back into the nail keg. "If'n it break, oonuh can't peddle hit." He turned on his heel and picked up his hat as he limped through the backdoor of the store to the dock.

Using his walking stick, Samuel lowered himself into the blue rowboat, untied the rope from the cleat, lit his pipe, and moved into the current of the rising tide. The boat glided toward the setting sun. Samuel rowed with his back to the bow, his strong arms and shoulders working easily.

Two large buzzards circled overhead in the cloudless sky. This late afternoon trip back home along the Sampit was a favorite part of his day. Fading sunlight glittered across the water, stirred by Samuel's oars.

He drifted and thought.

The pleasant meetings with Mayor Morgan and Miz Pringle and the conflict with Richard Meade rolled through his mind. The contrast between the three encounters illustrated the way life had been all of these years. For Samuel, who had the gift of second sight, few people were purely good, few people were all bad. Most people had some of both. That was true of Mayor Morgan, Miz Pringle, and Richard Meade.

Around the big bend in the river, Samuel rested his oars again. The sky was red, and orange, and pink with the last traces of day. On the far bank, he watched a massive alligator slide into the dark water for the night. A fish leapt from the river ahead of the big reptile.

At his dock near the Gullah Line, Samuel lit his corncob pipe again. He watched the tide turn, carrying the flotsam of the day back toward

Winyah Bay. The sweeping beam of the lighthouse passed overhead. Across the sandy tract, the light was on in Maggie Howard's kitchen.

Bet she got some t'in' good to eat, he thought.

Through the window, he saw Maggie serving supper to Sally. He wished he could eat supper with them, but not tonight. Not tonight.

Chapter Eight

Professor Rosen:

Hanukkah dates back to 164 B.C.E. Hanukkah means dedication. It commemorates a miracle. It is an eight-day festival of thanksgiving and rededication for the Jewish community.

Antiochus Epiphanes, a Syrian with a Greek name, was a harsh and cruel tyrant. Under Antiochus, Jewish worship, including the observance of Passover and the Sabbath, was forbidden. An idol of the Greek god Zeus was set up in the Temple, and the scrolls of the Torah were burned. Antiochus slaughtered a pig on the altar of the Temple, committing what the Prophet Daniel referred to as the "abomination of desecration." The Greek-Syrians murdered thousands of Jewish dissidents who remained steadfastly loyal to the Jewish faith.

Under the leadership of Yehuda, the Hammer, better known as Judas Maccabee, the Jews defeated an army of 40,000 Syrians. Judas and the Maccabees liberated Jerusalem. They entered the Temple and cleared it of idols. They built and dedicated a new altar to replace the one desecrated by Antiochus.

A part of the dedication was the relighting of the eternal flame, representing the presence of God in the Temple. According to Talmudic tradition, there was only enough consecrated olive oil to keep the light burning for one day. By Jewish law, eight days were required to consecrate new oil. Miraculously, the small cruse of oil burned for eight days.

The Hanukkah menorah is a nine-branched lampstand. The branch in the center is usually slightly elevated or distinguished in some way from the other eight branches. The elevated branch holds the *Shamash*, the servant light, the center candle used to light the other candles. The eight remaining candles correspond to each successive night of Hanukkah. They represent the eight-day miracle of Hanukkah.

As a devout Jew, Eli Solomon observed Hanukkah even in the isolation of North Island.

Tuesday, December 19, 1916 – Hanukkah begins at sundown.

The first year Eli was on North Island, he started a vegetable garden. The salt-laden sand was not suitable for growing anything other than sandspurs, grasses, and other vegetation natural to the barrier island. So, at a level place near the forest, he built raised beds from driftwood.

The plot received full sun throughout the day. Building up suitable soil required intensive labor. Except on the Sabbath, Eli had made regular trips to the freshwater ponds at the interior of the island. He carried with him two large pails and returned with rich topsoil. It took several months to transfer enough to fill the raised beds. For Eli, the results were worth the effort.

By early summer, the seeds he had saved from the previous year's garden were bearing fruit: tomatoes, squash, green beans, lima beans, and sweet corn. On his grandfather's farm in the old country, he had learned to grow beets, potatoes, peas, cabbage, kale, and lettuce in the fall and winter. Eli's garden supplied some kind of vegetable year-round. Even in December, cabbage, collards, mustard greens, lettuce, onions, and parsley were growing.

In the early spring, Eli dug in the decomposed goat manure that had seasoned in the sun. He planted seeds that he had saved from the year before. He mulched his vegetables with pine straw gathered from beneath the nearby loblolly pines. Every year he added another vegetable variety and a few garden flowers just for their beauty.

Each day, Eli sprinkled the urine he collected in the pickle jar all around the perimeter of the garden. He examined the vegetable plants for insect pests and added some pine straw. His work in the garden was an act of reverence.

To tend a garden, thought Eli, *is to be a partner with God.*

For Eli, the garden was an expression of faith; working in the garden was an act of prayer. Much like keeping kosher, tending the garden was a part of his spiritual path.

Now, in the hot, dry air of December, his winter garden was wilting and would be gone if rain did not come. The lettuce was already withered. Root crops like onions, turnips, and carrots might recover if rain came soon. Eli could not use water from the cistern for the garden, and hauling water from the pond took too much time. He used the leftover water from his weekly bath, clothes washing, and mopping to nourish the garden. Just a few hardy herbs remained healthy in the garden that had been so generous to him all spring and summer. Perhaps it was time for the garden to rest. Even the soil needed *Shabbes,* Sabbath rest.

This Tuesday, the beginning of Hanukkah, was a day of work and a day of celebration. Before long, Inspector Roy Holden would make his quarterly visit, but probably not until after December 25. Eli still had much to do to make sure the government property was well maintained. The observance of Hanukkah would begin at sundown. But, first, there were several tasks to complete.

After Eli had painted the skiff, he touched up a few other places in need of white paint. He had meticulously cleaned his paintbrushes using turpentine to soften the bristles. They were just about worn out.

He made a note to ask Officer Roy Holden for new ones when Officer Holden came for the inspection. For now, the older brushes would have to do. It was time to touch up places where the paint had chipped away. This was especially important to prevent rust on metal parts.

The Pink Book included an entire section entitled "How to Paint." The lighthouse keeper was expected to keep everything on government property well maintained. Painting was a big part of the job. The tower itself had to be painted regularly. That task consumed a lot of time. Eli had painted the entire eighty-seven-foot tower in the spring and early summer before the storms came. He had to suspend himself from the railing above with a thick rope tied in a double bowline. That gave him a secure seat. He braced his feet against the tower wall, held the paint on his lap secured by a rope over his left shoulder, and painted above his head with his right hand. It was a backbreaking task that took two months to complete.

On Monday he had painted the skiff white and had touched up a few places with the same paint. Today he needed to paint several more places, this time with different colors. *The Pink Book* was specific:

"In using the brush, where there is sufficient space, long strokes should be employed to extend the color in a smooth and uniform manner; where the space is contracted or rough, the paint should be laid on in dabs, for the purpose of getting it into the recesses and places where the surface is unequal."

The colors to be used were also specified. On the outside, white was applied to all wooden structures. Trim work was to be red. Black paint was used for the lantern room, the galley railings, and the handrails along the tower steps. All other iron structures were to be primed with red leaded paint and then with brown paint. Outside shutters were to be dark green. Red was rarely used except to mark the starboard side on docks and channel markings. Whitewash was to be used on stone and brick work and on rough-board work.

Inside painting was no less specific. White was used for the interior of the lantern room, and for all interior woodwork except hardwood. Green was the color for tables, chairs, and all other furniture. Iron staircases and railings were to be primed and painted black. Even the underside of the tower stairs had to be painted.

Heart pine floors and all hardwoods were not to be painted but were to be kept well-oiled or scrubbed. Whitewash could be used for interior walls, cellars, and outhouses, and any rough-board work when paint had not been authorized.

Using his brushes for the lighter colors first, Eli carefully cleaned the worn brushes with turpentine after each color was applied. As he applied black paint to the railings along the stairway inside the lighthouse, he cleaned cobwebs from the crevices where the iron rails were attached to the wall of the tower.

Near the bottom of the stairs, he brushed away a cobweb with his left hand. As he did, he felt something crawling on his thumb. It was a large black widow spider. Instinctively, he brushed the venomous spider away with the paintbrush in his right hand. The spider fell to the floor, struggling with sticky paint on its body and legs. Eli paused to watch the tiny creature that was in obvious distress. He stepped outside the door of the lighthouse and picked up an oyster shell. Using the shell, he scooped up the spider, took it outside, and placed it at the base of the tall loblolly pine near the fuel shed.

He looked at his hand. Black paint smeared his left thumb, but he was unharmed by the black widow. The eight-legged creature had been minding her own business when Eli's hand brushed her from her web.

Now she was in peril. Eli wondered if she would live or if the oyster shell would be her final resting place.

For Eli, the episode was a reminder of the uncertain cycle of life and death. The drama played out in so many ways, large and small, the mystery of those who survive and those who do not. It had been the theme of Eli's life since the night of the fire in Odessa. He imagined it would always be so.

He returned to finish painting the railing in the tower, being a little more cautious as he brushed aside cobwebs.

Eli painted most of the day, stopping only for the noon meal, while Melchizedek kept the Nubians grazing on the dunes. By the end of the day, he put an asterisk by the note on his pad. He definitely needed a new paintbrush and a new stipple brush.

The sun was setting as he put the paint and the brushes away. He cleaned his hands, first with turpentine, then with soap and water. He applied more lanolin and grabbed the cloth bag before climbing the tower to light the lamp.

Alone in his transparent sanctuary, he watched the sky change colors from blue to pink to purple to deep indigo. Here there were no paintbrushes to clean up; here there was no strong turpentine odor. There were just vibrant colors, perfectly blended, painted on the canvas of the sky by the Creator.

Eli offered his evening prayers and struck an official match to light the double wicks. He dropped the torpedo weight, and the massive lens turned, casting light into the fading sky.

Back in the keeper's house, he prepared supper. The dog stretched out on the wooden floor, waiting to be fed. For this meal on the first night of Hanukkah, there would be no potato latkes and no applesauce, none of the traditional holiday fare. Eli fixed potatoes and apples fried in goat butter for himself. The dog would receive a generous piece of pork.

When the food was ready, Eli took it to the table.

The dog jumped up but ran toward the door. He gave forth a low growl. Outside, the guinea fowl sounded the alarm from the live oak tree. Eli swung open the door and realized there was trouble at the goat pen. A pack of red wolves was trying to get to the Nubians. The dog gave a loud bark and rushed to the rescue. The wolves turned to face Melchizedek. Eli watched from the porch.

Eli had rarely seen the wolves. They were nocturnal, even secretive in their behavior. The dog approached the pack steadily but slowly. To Eli's surprise, Melchizedek seemed bigger and taller than the largest wolf. But the dog's coat had the same red cast as the wolves. As the dog approached, the wolves, one by one, bowed, knelt, or lay down in the sand before him. The wolves clearly recognized Melchizedek as their superior. Slowly the dog positioned himself between the goats and the wolves. Then with one loud bark of authority from the dog, the wolves beat a hasty retreat up the island yelping as they fled.

Eli recalled that in the epic story of Abraham in the Torah, Melchizedek was referred to as both a priest and the king of Salem. Melchizedek, the dog, seemed also to play multiple roles.

Again, inside his house, Eli gave his dog, King Melchizedek, an extra ration of pork. Somewhere further up the island, the wolves howled at what was left of the waning moon.

As he ate the potatoes and apples, Eli recalled the story of Hanukkah, shared with him by his parents and grandparents. It was a story of freedom from tyranny, of light, and hope overcoming hate and fear. It was the central Jewish narrative from the exodus out of bondage in Egypt to the liberation from exile in Babylon. It was a story he would have told Lenora had she lived.

Eli remembered these events important to his faith. He recalled, too, the happy family celebrations of Hanukkah, the good food, and the candles in the window. The words of his grandfather summarizing Jewish history came to mind.

They tried to destroy us. We survived. Let's have a feast.

Eli called to mind the pogroms in his native land. They were riots in which Jews were violently attacked and persecuted. Soldiers and police often looked on from a safe distance without interfering. Whether or not the czarist government-organized pogroms, the government's anti-Semitic policies certainly encouraged them. The persecution resulted in the emigration of thousands of Ukrainian Jews to the United States. Among those immigrants was Eli's uncle Mordecai.

Eli's parents and his grandparents had all died before Eli's home was burned, and his wife and his child were lost. He had no reason to remain in Odessa, so he decided to follow his uncle to America.

He was still a young man, only twenty-two years old when he left his native Ukraine and made the long pilgrimage to find his uncle. The journey was complicated. He first entered Canada and then made his way to South Carolina. His Uncle Mordecai had introduced him to the Jewish community in Georgetown. It was there that he met Heiman Kaminski. Mr. Kaminski had given Eli his first job in America, working in the hardware store.

Today was the first day of Hanukkah. The observance began at sundown. Eli was deeply grateful for his Jewish heritage. His heart's desire was to be an observant Jew. His work at the North Island lighthouse made that difficult. The rabbi at Temple Beth Israel explained that his work was included in a provision known as *pikkuah nefesh*. Most Jewish laws may be suspended to save a life. Rescuing a life in danger takes precedence over the Sabbath. The work of a lighthouse keeper certainly qualified.

He wondered, again, about the fate of the black widow spider.

Eli wanted to be observant as far as possible. It was the reason he had carved a mezuzah from cedar for his front door. The rabbi had blessed it and had given Eli the tiny scroll to place inside. Eli had also crafted a homemade menorah from driftwood found on the beach.

Eli lit the first candle as soon after sundown as he could. He placed the menorah in a window in the keeper's house so the light could be seen by those passing the house. On North Island, there were few to pass by except Eli, the dog, the goats, the guinea fowl, and maybe a few other creatures.

The candles served as a reminder to Eli of God's power. Each night as he lit the candles, he would recite the simple Hebrew blessing. On this first night, there were three blessings.

Blessed are You, Lord our God,
King of the Universe,
Who has sanctified us with His commandments
and commanded us to kindle the light of Hanukkah.
Blessed are You, Lord our God,
King of the Universe,
Who performed miracles for our fathers in those days,
and at this time.

Blessed are You, Lord our God,
Ruler of the universe,
Who has given us life, sustained us,
and brought us to this season.

בָּרוּךְ אַתָּה יְיָ, אֱלֹהֵינוּ מֶלֶךְ הָעוֹלָם,

Chapter Nine

Professor Rosen:

Following the Civil War, the recently freed slaves in Georgetown elected Joseph Hayne Rainey as the first African-American to serve in Congress. Georgetown was unusual in that in 1879, Blacks and whites settled on a political compromise known as Fusion. The plan allowed for the sharing of political influence across the color line. Fusion kept racial peace in Georgetown for more than two decades because all of the African-American officeholders during that time were local citizens. Northerners who came south after the Civil War for personal gain, also known as Carpetbaggers and Scalawags, were absent from Georgetown politics.

In other parts of the state of South Carolina, racial hatred was marked by the rise of the Ku Klux Klan. The KKK was a white supremacy organization imported from Tennessee in 1868. It was anti-Semitic as well as an advocate for violence against Blacks. The Klan wave of terror in the Palmetto State, especially in the Upstate, resulted in federal intervention by President Ulysses S. Grant in 1871. The KKK trials in Columbia, in which five Klansmen were charged, began in November of 1871. Five white men on trial were convicted and sentenced for crimes against Black citizens.

When Governor Ben Tillman took office in 1890, the disenfranchisement of African-Americans in South Carolina became permanent. In 1895 the state constitution was rewritten, effectively eliminating the right of black citizens to vote. Though never officially ratified, it became *de facto* law.

In 1901, President Theodore Roosevelt invited Booker T. Washington to dine with him in the White House. As a result, South Carolina Senator Tillman roared from the United States Senate floor, "The action of President Roosevelt in entertaining that nigger will necessitate our killing a thousand niggers in the South before they learn their place again."

Throughout the racial turmoil in other parts of the state, Georgetown had enjoyed racial harmony for twenty-four years. That ended on Front Street on Saturday, September 29, 1900. Deputy Sheriff J. C. Scurry stopped by John Brownfield's barbershop to collect the poll tax. Brownfield, a Black man, shot and killed Scurry, a white man. Brownfield was arrested and put in the local jail. Rumors spread that white citizens intended to lynch Brownfield. The next day, Sunday, more than one thousand Blacks walked through the streets shouting, "Save John." Some carried pitchforks and rice hooks. The Georgetown Rifle Guards were held in readiness but were not used.

The protest continued on Monday while the mayor met with civic leaders representing both races. Finally, the mayor wired the Governor for help. Four armed companies of the state guard arrived the next day, bringing with them several Gatling guns. The troops paraded through the town on Tuesday morning. That same day six women and three men, all African-Americans identified as leaders in the demonstrations, were tried and convicted in a Mayor's court. All were found guilty. The women were ordered to pay fines. The men were given time on the chain gang. John Brownfield never went to trial. He later committed suicide in his jail cell.

The peaceful solution of Fusion in Georgetown was dead.

In his book *The Nature of Prejudice,* Harvard psychologist Gordon Allport identified fear as the underlying cause of prejudice. It was a truth that Samuel Pringle knew all too well.

Tuesday, December 19, 1916, continued

The hot and dry weather of December was oppressive and disorienting. Christmas was less than a week away, but the people of Georgetown County acted as if were the middle of summer. People sat in the shade, drinking lemonade to escape the afternoon heat. Women carried parasols; men wore straw hats; palmetto palm fans were in high demand.

The purple martins and swallows had long since flown south for the winter. Dragonflies had pretty much run their course, so voracious mosquitoes, biting flies, and ubiquitous black gnats were abundant along the banks of the Sampit River.

Visitors from other climes fanned the gnats casually with an open hand or swatted at them with unleashed fury. Lowcountry folks didn't raise a hand. Instead, they had developed a particular way, unique to the area, of dispersing the tiny pests. Their method was called puffing. By protruding the lower lip and blowing upward in short bursts, the gnats could be held at bay. Puffing gnats was an acquired skill, learned from childhood.

Samuel Pringle arrived early for work at Meade's General Store as he did every Tuesday, the day when supplies to restock the store arrived. The delivery wagon pulled by a team of matched mules rolled down Front Street.

"Whoa, now," the teamster commanded, as the loaded buckboard stopped in front of the store. The driver was Jasper, a young mulatto, no more than fifteen or sixteen years old, a lanky youth who was eager to work. Samuel admired his pleasant diligence.

123

"Mornin', Mr. Samuel," said Jasper. "Fetched a big load today."

"I see," replied Samuel.

"Christmas comin'. Folks buy more."

"Reckon so."

The two men unloaded supplies of rice, flour, cornmeal, and grits as well as several hands of burley tobacco and boxes of cigars. There was an assortment of washtubs and buckets, cast-iron skillets, Dutch ovens, and cooking pots as well as wooden kitchen implements. Also included were wooden cases of turpentine, linseed oil, and kerosene.

When Samuel saw the kerosene, he thought to himself, *Dat what Mr. Eli use way out on North Island to keep de lighthouse shinin'.*

Just as Jasper and Samuel finished unloading the wagon, Richard Meade appeared, criticizing how the supplies had been arranged in the store.

"By damn, leave it to a nigga' and a high yella' to make one hell of a mess."

The lad handed Meade a piece of paper. "Suh, dis da bill o' laden."

"You can be sure I'll check behind you two ne'r-do-wells carefully in case you stole something from me."

"We ain't stole nothin', suh," said Samuel, removing his hat and mopping his face and head with the bandana.

"Don't you back sass me, nigga'."

"Mr. Samuel, I be back next Tuesday, day after Christmas," said Jasper climbing to the seat of the empty wagon. He popped the reins, "Git up, now."

"Well, well, Mr. Samuel is it? You ain't nothin' but a sorry nigga', the wretched of the earth."

Samuel turned and looked Meade in the eye. Richard Meade's bulging eyes narrowed to thin slits in a fiery crimson face. His soul was filled with fear and with hate. For a brief moment, the two men were locked in intense eye contact.

"Nigga', what are you looking at?"

"Suh, have oonuh heard from oonuh daughter?"

"Hell, no," he shouted. "She's been in New York for more than a week now. My wife is worried sick about her way up there with all them Yankees, Jews, Roman Catholics, and carpetbaggers. There is not one damn person up there that we can trust, not even our girl."

Meade turned away, his back toward Samuel. Composing himself, he wheeled back around to face Samuel, "What business is my daughter to you anyway?"

Samuel turned away, feeling sorry for Richard Meade. The man had so much to be thankful for: a good business, a fine family. But fear ruled the man to the point that he had no peace, no comfort, and no respect for others, not even for himself.

Meade spoke, "If it weren't for that Jew, Heiman Kaminski, my daughter would have never thought about going to New York. If he had stuck with shipping lumber instead of opening that Clyde Line franchise, my child would be here with her mama where she's supposed to be. I can't believe I had to pay good money to that Jew to take her away from us off to that godforsaken place, and at Christmas, of all times. The steamer *Cherokee* is supposed to be back in Georgetown two days before Christmas Day. Kaminski damn well better get her home safely."

Red-faced and frustrated, Richard Meade turned to leave. "I'm going to the bank and home to eat. Nigga', you watch the place while I'm gone. If you sell something, leave the money on the counter. Don't go near the cash drawer."

When Richard Meade left for the bank, Samuel pulled down a bolt of red calico cloth from the shelf. With his jackknife, he cut off an eight-inch strip from the end of the fabric. Returning the material to its proper place, he selected an asafetida bag from a box under the counter. He found a nickel in his pocket and placed it on the counter in payment for the small bag. The calico strip and the bag went deep into his overall pockets.

Samuel walked to the back of the store. He stood in the dockside doorway of Meade's General Store, mopping his brow with a faded red bandana and puffing black gnats. When he was satisfied that no one was watching, he urinated from the dock into the Sampit River. Back inside the long hallway he paused to take a drink of water.

A narrow rustic hunter's table held two enameled buckets of water, one marked with a sign that read "For White Only," the other marked "colored." At the end of each workday, water from the white bucket was poured into the colored bucket. Each morning Richard Meade brought fresh water in the white bucket with him from his home. The white bucket was equipped with a shiny new dipper. A brown dipping gourd sufficed for the colored bucket. Samuel drank from the gourd.

He again wiped the sweat from his face with the faded bandana and returned to his work stocking the supplies that had come in that morning. When Richard Meade returned from the noon meal at his house, he was no less vexed than he had been before he left.

"Has there been a telegram delivery?"

"No, suh, no telegram."

"Damn, I wished that girl would let us know she was safe."

Samuel didn't respond.

"Any sales while I was gone?"

"Jest one sale. Sell a'fidity bag. Nickel on da counter."

"It must be this heat. Nobody's buying. Bank teller said things are slow for everybody. Good thing I have the Lighthouse Service contract. Kaminski tried to outbid me on that, but I lowballed him. At least I beat him at something. Besides that inspector, what's his name? Holden. Officer Roy Holden can't abide Jews."

Samuel thought, *Officer Roy Holden and Richard Meade be a lot alike.*

"Isn't it about time for that lighthouse keeper to come into town?"

"Yes, suh, nearly 'bout time."

"I can't fathom the Federal Government giving a job like that to a damn Jew. They might as well have given it to a nigga' like you."

Samuel didn't respond.

"Why is nobody buying anything? The whole damn town is decorated for Christmas. All up and down Front Street. Back over in the neighborhoods, some already have a Christmas tree up. My wife is ready for a tree. Wonder where I could get one?"

"Jasper. He sell cedars. Cut'em near the Sampit Swamp."

"How can I find him?"

"He done be here t'day, mabbe still in town. Keep eye out fo'em."

Samuel Pringle spent the rest of the afternoon straightening and cleaning the store. It was a low-paying job, not like the time he worked for the lumber mill. But it wasn't like working as a slave on the rice plantation either. Samuel was glad to have work, even if Richard Meade was his boss. Being able to work at all, crippled as he was, gave him a reason to row his boat in to Georgetown every day. Doing his work well was a matter of pride for him, a source of dignity.

It was nearly closing time when Samuel heard the distinctive sounds of Jasper's wagon and his mules. He went to the front door and flagged Jasper.

"Whoa, now," Jasper said to his team.

"Mr. Meade, want see oonah."

Meade pushed Samuel aside, approaching Jasper. "My nigga' says you sell Christmas trees. That right?"

"Yes, suh. Red cedars cut outta' Sampit Swamp."

"What do you charge?"

"Two-bits a foot."

"I need a ten-foot tree," said Meade.

"Only one left today is dis little one," Jasper said, motioning to the last cedar in the wagon. I gots to haul a load to Andrews in da' mornin'. I be bring a ten-foot come Friday, day afta' t'morrow."

"Come by here," Meade said. "We'll take it to my house."

"I'll cut at fust light, and den come to town."

"See you then."

Samuel waved at Jasper.

Jasper said, "Mr. Samuel, can oonuh do wit a little scrub tree?"

"Sho' can."

"Come git it. It oonuh's."

Samuel took the small tree from the wagon. It was not as tall as Samuel, not as tall as the one from which John Howard made Samuel's walking stick, but it was a Christmas tree, all right.

"Much obliged, Jasper."

"Welcome, Mr. Samuel. Gotta go." He popped the reins, "Git on now."

As the wagon pulled away, Samuel admired his tree. It was small, but it was a pretty little tree.

Be jest right for Maggie and Sally, he thought.

Samuel hobbled with the tree through the store toward the dock out back.

"Nigga', did you pay good money for that scruffy twig? At twenty-five cents a foot that must have set you back a dollar. That's two days' pay for you. You've got more money than you've got sense. Besides, you can't trust a high yella', none of them."

Without a word, Samuel carried the little tree to his boat out back, pleased that he had something to give Maggie and Sally.

He finished sweeping the store and the street out front with a broom he had made. He put it away, retrieved his hat from the nail at the backdoor, and left out of the front door. Even at quitting time, it was still hot and dry.

Walking down Front Street, he admired the Christmas decorations. Some were simple arrangements, a few magnolia leaves and a ribbon. Others were more elaborate with mixed evergreens: magnolia, holly, yellow pine, and red cedar and accented with bright red apples, lemons, pears, and pineapples.

Most all de people of Georgetown are good folks, Samuel thought. *Some say one bad apple can spoil de whole bunch, but dat weren't true in Georgetown.*

There were some bad apples, but most everybody Samuel knew was good. He limped, using his walking stick, past the jewelry store where the Jewish people used to meet upstairs for services every Friday night.

Samuel passed shops and stores all the way to the Old Market. This was where slaves had been bought and sold. It was the same building where John Brownfield was put in jail after he shot the sheriff's deputy. It was where Brownfield died in his cell by his own hand.

At Kaminski Hardware, he turned toward the river, hobbling along until he came to his blue boat. Slowly he rowed up the Sampit to his simple cypress dock on the Gullah Line. This was a favorite part of the day for Samuel. To be on the river at dusk was peaceful. A screech owl broke the stillness calling from the low branch of a live oak draped in Spanish moss.

Dis hot spell ain't natural, he thought. *Gonna' be a storm 'fo long.*

He tied up the boat to the cleat on his dock. He paused to light his pipe. He walked toward Maggie's house, moving awkwardly, balancing with the tree in one hand and his walking stick in the other. He saw her through an open window tending to Sally. He moved closer to the house and felt a flutter in his stomach, excited about giving a present to a good-looking woman.

Samuel paused to knock the ashes from his pipe. On second thought, why waste the tobacco? He took the pretty little tree and leaned it against the porch of a special lady. He was sure she would find it. She might even know who gave it to her.

Though he was old and though he had lost his manhood in the accident at the lumber mill, he wondered. *How could an old fella' like him git so stirred up 'bout a fine woman like Maggie?* That night he dreamed about her.

Chapter Ten

Professor Rosen:

During the 1700s, Georgetown was a busy commercial port. A lighthouse was needed to guide ships into the harbor. It was decided to place the lighthouse on North Island, a fifteen-mile-long island just off the coast of Georgetown. In February of 1795, the government bought land for the building of a lighthouse tower. Construction was delayed, but in 1799 the first Georgetown Light on North Island was completed. It was a wooden structure that was seventy-two feet tall, twenty-six feet in diameter at the base, and six feet in diameter at the top.

The first lighthouse was destroyed by a storm in 1804 and was replaced in 1812 by a new tower. It also was seventy-two feet tall, but this one was made of brick and was painted white. This light was damaged severely during the Civil War when Confederate troops used explosives to destroy the top of the tower so it could not be used by advancing Union forces.

The tower that stands today replaced the 1812 tower and was completed in 1867. This new structure was eighty-seven feet tall with a base diameter of twenty feet and a base wall thickness of six inches. It was equipped with a fourth-order Fresnel lens. Other buildings included an fuel shed and a wooden keeper's house with a cistern and a privy. The existing Georgetown Light is the third lighthouse tower to be built on North Island, South Carolina. Eli Solomon was the first Jewish keeper of the light.

Wednesday, December 20, 1916

Eli Solomon stood atop the lighthouse tower on North Island gazing at the calm blue-green water of the Atlantic Ocean. He watched the osprey take flight from her perch in the tall loblolly near the fuel shed. The magnificent bird glided effortlessly above the waves. When she spotted a mullet near the surface, the raptor plunged feetfirst into the water, sinking sharp talons into the fish, then turning the catch in the direction of her flight. Alighting on the pine perch, she enjoyed her freshly caught breakfast.

As the rising sun emerged from the sea, Eli extinguished the lamp and offered his morning prayers. He paused to give thanks for his job.

The daily routine of a lighthouse keeper was demanding and constant, even on a good day. The repetitive tasks might be tedious for some people, but not for Eli. The property had to be maintained, the log had to be updated, and the lamp had to be burning from sunset to sunrise.

Still, there were plenty of diversions. Observing the sea birds along the Atlantic and the shorebirds along the bay was a pleasant pastime. Paying attention to the varied wildlife of North Island was fascinating. Identifying the plants growing on the dunes, in the marsh, and in the woods was interesting to the Ukrainian transplant. He looked forward to the migratory birds, especially the bobolinks. They returned every year to feast on what was left of the rice fields, singing a happy song as they gleaned the grain.

Even the isolation of the place was comfortable for the lighthouse keeper. The solitude and the opportunity to live near the sea were special benefits to his job. Eli had always lived near the sea. The sea was filled with life and was life-giving. Fishing was a pleasant way to spend time and supplement his dietary needs. He enjoyed the rolling waves, the ocean breeze, and the changing season of his new home. Of course, it was past time for the season to change, but he knew that it would sooner or later.

The sheer beauty and wildness of his island home enriched his life. Living here and working at the lighthouse was a privilege, even a blessing for the keeper. Knowing that he was rendering a service for his new country and for those who depended on him was fulfilling. On those times when he had saved a life, he felt it was an honor to hold this position.

Eli needed the job for the same reason most people were employed; to earn a living. It rewarded him with a place to live and funds sufficient to meet his needs. Despite what some of his detractors thought of him, Meade and Holden to name two, the vocation of a lighthouse keeper was an honorable profession. The work gave Eli a sense of dignity.

There were other benefits as well – a herd of Nubians, a fine dog, a flock of Guineas, and a good friend like Samuel. His persistent regret was that he could not be as faithful to his Jewish tradition as he would have liked.

He looked in the other direction across Winyah Bay. On this bright sunny day he saw two boats trawling the water off of Cat Island. They were in search of shrimp. Using haul seines, mesh nets pulled by their rowboats through shallow waters, they hoped to find shrimp, even this late in the season. As he watched them, he noticed that they seemed to be having some luck.

He recalled fishing with his father and his grandfather. They usually trolled for sturgeon because the Russian appetite for caviar brought a good income for Jewish families. But the best, the beluga and the starlet sturgeons were not always easy to find. More often than not, the fishermen had to trawl for smaller varieties like anchovies, shad, smelt, or mullet. Much like shrimping on Winyah Bay, seining with nets was hard labor that demanded long hours. Unless they caught sturgeon, the effort offered little more than subsistence living.

The seaport of Odessa has a long history. It was said to have been built on the site of an ancient Greek colony. Because it was such a desirable harbor, it had been occupied through its early history by Crimea, Turkey, and Lithuania. The Russian Empire founded a city in 1794 as a naval fortress.

The old people of Odessa remembered a legend that the city was renamed Odessa by Queen Catherine II. The Czarina was not a native Russian. She wanted the beautiful city to have a feminine name. She changed the Greek *Odessos* to the feminine Odessa, referring to the city as the Pearl of the South.

Another legend held that the name Odessa came from a play on words in French, the language of the Russian court. *Assez d'eau* means enough of water. If the French word is mispronounced, that is, spoken backwards, it sounds similar to the Greek colony's name. The water-related pun makes perfect sense, because Odessa, though situated next to the Black Sea, has a limited supply of fresh water.

Eli's grandfathers, both of them, recalled the Crimean War of 1853–56. During the war Odessa was bombarded by British and French warships. It soon recovered and became Russia's largest grain-exporting port.

Eli was born and reared in the city of Odessa, located on a hill above the Black Sea. When Eli was not fishing with his father and grandfather, he worked at the docks loading grain. He was certain that dock work in Odessa had prepared him for his first job in Georgetown. He loaded tall ships at the lumber mill. Yellow pine lumber from South Carolina had been shipped up and down the east coast. The light keeper's house on North Island was built from heart pine lumber cut from the forest in Georgetown County.

Odessa had a lighthouse, too. In fact, the Georgetown Light reminded Eli of the Vorontsov Lighthouse. Like the North Island light, the first light in Odessa was built entirely of wood. The current Vorontsov Light built in 1888 was two feet taller than the Georgetown Light. The Odessa lighthouse was connected with the port's shoreline by a long stone causeway, called the Quarantine and Road jetties. Both jetties protected the port from the high seas coming from the South. The jetties that protected the entry to Winyah were no less impressive.

The first lighthouse near Odessa was constructed in 1827 at Big Fountain Cape. Eli's father had told him the tragic story behind the decision to build that first wooden tower. A landowner made a bonfire on the seacoast. The captain of a passing trade ship mistook the fire for harbor lights and sailed his boat into the rocks along the coast. The boat ran aground, and one of the sailors was killed. The landowner had such remorse about the tragedy that he gave his land to a monastery. The one condition for the gift was that a lighthouse would be built on the site.

As he went through the routine of the day, preparing the government property for an inspection, Eli considered another trip up the island to the freshwater pond. He really didn't want another high adventure with animals reacting so oddly in this unseasonably hot weather. He put off the decision to another time. North Island needed rain. Eli was sure it would come. It always had.

His morning reflections on life in Odessa had made him homesick for the Black Sea, for potato latkes for Hanukkah, for another person to speak to him in Yiddish or even in the Ukrainian language. Most of all, he longed for a family to embrace. After twenty-one years, he still grieved.

After supper of bread and cheese, Eli walked to the tower. It was just past dusk. Though he was a little late to his task, he paused to admire the sky. The moon showed only a faint sliver, a fingernail moon his wife had called it. When the date for Hanukkah was established, it was done so the midpoint of the celebration would always fall on the dark of the moon. In the midst of Hanukkah, the sky is the darkest of the month of Kislev. That is the reason Hanukkah is called the Festival of Lights. Gazing into the night, before lighting the lamp in the tower, Eli noticed the stars shining brightly in the dark canopy above.

All of heaven is celebrating Hanukkah, Eli thought.

With the double wicks of the lamp lighted and evening prayers said, Eli descended the tower. The dog had herded the goats into their pen. Eli latched the gate behind them. The Guinea fowl were roosting. The howl of a wolf moaned from somewhere up the island. The dog turned his head in the direction of the sound and trotted up the path beyond the garden into the woods.

Eli let him go without interference.

Inside the house, Eli lit two candles in the menorah giving the traditional blessing. He rolled into his hammock to sleep with Odessa on his mind, his parents and grandparents, his wife and daughter. He missed them all. Soon he was asleep.

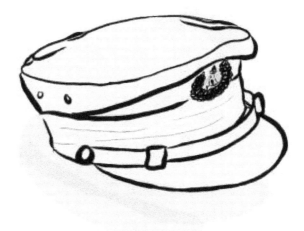

Chapter Eleven

Professor Rosen:

The storm of 1893 was especially memorable. On August 27, the winds started blowing, the seas churning. The storm struck near Savannah, Georgia. The winds there were 120 miles per hour, tearing houses apart. Storm waves were estimated at sixteen feet high, putting the islands off Beaufort under water.

The 1893 storm, the Sea Islands Hurricane, is considered one of the deadliest in American history. An estimated 2,000 people died, and tens of thousands were left with nothing but their lives. It might have been even worse than that. Most of the people living on those islands were poor, Black workers from the rice fields.

Telegraph service was new to the South, but the people living on the islands had neither forewarning nor any access to the news.

A report from L.N. Jesunofsky, an observer for the Charleston Weather Bureau on August 28, 1893, read:

> Passing from the Battery on the East Side of Charleston to the northward, the scene of wreckage which meets the eye is desolate in the extreme. All piers on the east side are stripped bare, the sheds being leveled. Three are total wrecks. Many commercial and pleasure crafts are broken in pieces, literally ground up by the fury of waves and wind. The streets all over the city are strewn with debris. Seventy-five percent of all telephone, telegraph, and electric lights are completely

down. Large trees are lying across the streets, roofs are entirely bare.

Anne Weston Smoak of Magnolia Beach, near Pawleys Island, survived by clinging for hours to a cedar tree outside her home. With the ocean roiling so ferociously around her, she feared at one point that the tree would be swept out to sea.

Forty years later she gave this account to the *Charleston News and Courier*.

> The forty-foot waves soon claimed Dr. Arthur Flagg, his wife Elizabeth, and Pauline Weston. Each one left, fighting for life, cruelly beaten by the waves. The writer was twice knocked from the small limb to which she was clinging, but catching the tip end of it, she pulled herself back in spite of floating boards, furious seas, and sand-laden winds cutting flesh like sharp pieces of glass.

Dr. Flagg's body was found and identified by his vest and his gold pocket watch. His wife's sister, Pauline Weston, was discovered still clutching the tiny body of the Flagg's baby, both Aunt and child perished by drowning.

The hurricane of 1893 was the last in a series of three major storms in a single decade that destroyed the rice plantations. When rice fields were flooded with seawater, the crop died because salt water kills the plants. After three attempts to start over, the plantation owners were financially destitute. During this period, many sold their land. The golden age of Carolina Gold rice was ended.

It was also the time that a plan to construct jetties at the mouth of Winyah Bay was put forward. The jetties were completed in 1904 at a cost of more than $7 million dollars.

Eli Solomon was grateful for the jetties for more than one reason. Not only did they protect the entrance to Winyah Bay, they also provided attractive cover for fish that were a good supplement to his diet. Fishing near the jetties was a happy diversion from the routine of a lighthouse keeper's life.

1916, the year of our story, was an active season. Fourteen tropical storms formed during the course of the year. Eleven hurricanes developed. Six of those were major hurricanes, all of them of category-three strength. A July hurricane sank *The Palmetto*, the private steamer yacht of Edwin Kaminski, eldest son of Heiman Kaminski.

The final storm of the season may have still been lurking somewhere out in the Atlantic.

Thursday, December 21, 1916

Eli took a moment to enjoy the view on a cloudless Thursday morning. From his vantage point atop the lighthouse, he noticed a tall ship under full sail off to the northeast. He was sure she was the lumber schooner *Waccamaw*, returning to the dock of the Atlantic Coast Lumber Company on the Sampit River. Eli judged she would come past the jetties into Winyah Bay shortly before sundown.

Eli watched in admiration as the Osprey plunged feet first into the waves, catching a small bluefish in its talons.

Maybe I will fish today, he thought.

The bird carrying its catch flew to a favorite perch, the tall loblolly pine near the oil shed. Eli had requested permission to remove the tree, fearing that in a storm, it might damage the building. Holden was annoyed with his persistence.

143

"Request denied." Roy Holden, the inspector for the lighthouse service, waved his hand and dismissed Eli matter-of-factly. "I've given you the same answer several times. Don't ask me that again."

In the late afternoon, Eli walked to the beach, rod and reel in his left hand, cast net, and bucket in his right. He had spent his life near the sea. His father was a Ukrainian fisherman out of Odessa. In difficult times to provide for the family, he hired on as a dock worker loading wheat on large ships for export. But most of the time, he earned his livelihood fishing for sturgeon in the Black Sea. The sturgeon was not good to eat. They were ugly fish except to other sturgeons. Their only value was their unfertilized eggs, caviar, a Russian delicacy.

From the time he could swim, Eli's classroom became the boat. His teacher was his Papa. Eli learned his lessons well. Walking on the beach, near the north jetty, Eli saw birds flying above the ocean just beyond the breakers, a sure sign of baitfish in the water. "Birds above, fish below," he muttered to himself in his familiar Yiddish tongue.

He moved closer to the water's edge, the surf splashing against his legs. The ocean current swirling against the artificial barrier had carved out a deep hole in the sandy bottom. On the rising tide, fish that usually stayed in the deeper water beyond the breakers were swept into the hole. On the falling tide, some of the fish would be trapped in the deep pool.

The construction of the jetties was an enormous undertaking. The granite rocks that created the jetties had been hauled down the river to the mouth of the bay on barges. The stone barricades extended out into the Atlantic to keep the channel clear.

Those rocks also created cover for a variety of fish. For Eli, this deep hole was a favorite angling spot. Here he had caught sheepshead, bluefish, red drum, sea trout, and croaker. All found their way to his table.

He had also struggled here with sharks and, last June, had a fierce fight with a stingray.

According to Jewish dietary law, any aquatic animal without scales or fins is considered nonkosher, that is, Jews were not supposed to eat them. While shrimp, clams, oysters, mussels, and scallops were not permitted for Jews to eat, Eli did not think of avoiding them as deprivation. Rather, being kosher observant was a part of his spiritual path. He counted it as a joyful discipline.

Besides, a nonkosher sea creature on the end of a fishing line presented problems from the moment it was hooked. For example, to release a shark or a stingray usually required cutting the line.

Eli propped his rod and reel against a large piece of driftwood, a live oak sculptured by the surf and bleached in the sun. He crossed the dunes to the bay side to catch his bait.

As a boy, Eli had learned from his father how to use a cast net. "It is a skill that every fisherman should have," his father had taught him. "You can't catch fish without good bait."

Eli looped the draw rope around his left wrist and raised the large circle of the cast net before him. He spread the net, holding it at three points, one with his right hand, one with his left, and in between with his mouth. Gracefully, he turned in a pirouette, flinging the net into the bay as far as the rope allowed. With only a slight breeze, he was able to make a perfectly flat, circular cast. Eli waited while the lead weights pulled the net to the bottom. Then, quickly he pulled the draw rope, closing the net. He waited a few minutes before lifting the net from the water. Two dozen shad and several shrimp wiggled in their captivity. Eli tossed the shrimp back into the water. The shrimp would be suitable bait were he fishing for flounder, a tasty fish that was in the strictest sense kosher. Though flounder met the requirements of having fins and scales, some Jews regarded them as nonkosher because they are bottom feeders. Eli had occasionally eaten flounder, but today he was angling for bluefish. He selected six of the shad, dropping them in his bait bucket. The others he released to freedom in the bay.

The fisherman walked across the narrow neck of sand to the ocean side.

With a shad, he baited the hook on the braided line of his rod and reel. With the first cast, he placed the bait in the deep hole no more than a foot from the rocky reef and waited for his supper to bite.

The rhythm of the tide was soothing to Eli. The waves crashing against the rocks reminded him of the ocean's power. The smell of salt air and the wind in his face offered gentle blessings.

A glint in the sand to his left caught his eye. He thought it might be an unusual shell or a rock. Holding the rod high, he leaned down to pick up a sparkling green object in the surf. It was a piece of glass, thick and slightly curved. It had been polished smooth by the sand and the waves. Eli put it into his pocket. He knew just what he would do with the small treasure.

The lumber schooner, the *Waccamaw*, made her way into the channel between the jetties. The crew raised their hands in greeting as they entered the calm waters of the bay, leaving behind the rolling ocean waves. Eli knew the feeling well from his younger days in Odessa. A welcomed feeling of safety washes over any seafaring soul coming into harbor.

The *Waccamaw* was an impressive vessel, but not nearly as magnificent as her sister ship had been. *The City of Georgetown* was a four-masted schooner owned by sixty-three people, many of them citizens of

Georgetown. Others were investors from New England. The massive ship was launched in 1902, just one year after Eli had come to Georgetown. Eli had loaded lumber on the ship when he was still a dockworker for the Atlantic Coast Lumber Company.

The *City of Georgetown* sailed from Winyah Bay to New York regularly, easily carrying more than a half-million feet of yellow pine lumber.

Her owners and the residents of Georgetown were shocked to learn, in February 1913, that the schooner had collided with the passenger liner *Prinz Oskar* off the Delaware Capes. The schooner that was the pride of Georgetown sank, though all hands were rescued. As keeper of the lighthouse, Eli had been the last person in South Carolina to see the tall ship under sail.

Eli felt a tap, tap on his line, then a tug. He set the hook and began reeling in a fish that seemed about right for supper. He thought it might be a spot or a croaker until he saw a flash of blue. The bluefish fought against the pull of the braided line. Eli let the fish run and then begin slowly reeling in line.

Suddenly, the fish started swimming toward the beach. Eli reeled as fast as he could to take up the slack. He was surprised until he saw a gray dorsal fin cutting through the surf, bearing down on the bluefish. Now, the hooked fish erratically turned away from Eli, stripping line off the reel as he swam toward deeper water. And, then, a distinct bump. The hooked fish became dead weight. Eli reeled in the head of the bluefish. The shark had cut the catch in half.

Eli spoke to Melchizedek in Yiddish. "That was supper, but not for us. It was supper for the shark."

Eli selected another shad from the bucket. Again he made a perfect cast near the granite rocks of the jetty. He worked the shad into the deep pool. As he waited, he watched for the shark. He saw the dorsal fin rise in the waves further out. Then he remembered the story he had seen on the newspaper fragment about the great white shark that had killed four people and injured a fifth on the coast of New Jersey.

This shark is no great white, probably just a bull shark. There are enough bluefish for supper for both of us, Eli thought.

The afternoon sun was lower in the sky behind him. He saw the shark swim into the turbulent water between the north and south jetties. At that moment, Eli had a big strike on the end of his line. This time it was a much larger bluefish. The rod bent to the power of the fish. Line hummed from the reel. Finally, Eli was able to turn the large fish and work him toward the beach. The fish put up a valiant fight. Again, Eli's rod bent under the second run of the fish. And, again, Eli slowly cranked his prey toward the beach. The bluefish made two more spirited runs, both times taking line further out into the Atlantic.

After twenty minutes, Eli brought the exhausted fish into shallow water. It was the largest bluefish he had ever seen. Holding the line taut, the lighthouse keeper waded deeper into the surf. The big fish rested on the sand, top fins exposed, but gills still submerged.

Eli put his hand on the back of the fish. He patted him twice and spoke as only a fisherman speaks to a fish. "Good fight," he said in Yiddish, admiring his worthy opponent. "Now swim to freedom.

With that, Eli released the bluefish.

As he was putting another shad on the hook, a tremendous wave crashed on the jetty. The impact sounded like a clap of thunder. Ocean spray drenched Eli. He waited for a moment before casting again.

Just one massive wave. It was an alarm, a sure signal. Eli was certain. For those who understood the ocean, the wave was the way the sea warned that a storm was about three days away. It was known as a prophet wave, the forerunner of a storm.

On the third cast, Eli hooked a smaller bluefish. *This one will fit into my pan.*

He landed the fish easily. He dumped the remaining shad into the surf, half-filled his bucket with fresh seawater, and cleaned the fish using the driftwood as a cutting board. He cut the fish into pan-sized filets, filled the bucket again with fresh seawater, and put the pieces of fish into the brine to soak. This would remove some of the oil and blood from the bluefish.

Black-faced laughing gulls gathered nearby to claim the remains of the fish. With the cleaned fish fillets in the bucket, Eli turned back to the house carrying his fishing gear. Just then, he saw a perfectly formed calico scallop. He put the bucket down and picked up the shell rinsing it in the surf. He examined the small treasure. It certainly deserved a place on the windowsill. With the shell secure in his shirt pocket, he picked up the bucket and walked back over the dunes.

On the way to the keeper's house, Eli made a detour past his vegetable garden to gather a few sprigs of rosemary. The garden was wilting almost before his eyes

As he circled the dry garden, he saw something that startled him. Between the garden and the woods, he noticed an indentation in the dry sand. He stooped to examine a single track. At first, he thought it might be the paw print of a large bear. But it was not. It was the unmistakable print of a large, bare human foot. He searched the surrounding area for more evidence of a visitor. There were no other footprints, but he could see that coming out of the woods to the edge of his garden, the sand had been disturbed. Another person had come near.

Eli stood up. His eyes searched the woods in the fading afternoon sun. He thought he saw movement in the undergrowth between the live oaks, palmettos, and pines, but he was not sure. Cold chills ran up his spine. He continued to look deep into the forest but saw nothing unusual. He looked again at the print in the sand. There was no doubt. It had been made by the bare foot of another person. The print was unusually large. Eli could easily fit his own boot inside the footprint.

Whoever left the print must be a giant, he thought.

When he reached the kitchen, he built a small fire inside the wood-burning stove. After sundown, he would grill the bluefish. Bread and water would complete his evening meal.

The large wave that crashed on the jetty signaled a powerful disturbance at sea. Eli had heard a prophet wave before, three other times that very summer, each time ahead of a gale. It was one of the ways he knew to anticipate an approaching storm. This one should arrive late Sunday or early Monday. That would give him time to get into Georgetown and back on Friday before Shabbes began at sundown.

According to ship captains, 1916 had been an unusually active hurricane season along the Atlantic coast. Eli was aware of three that had come near North Island.

A storm with strong winds came ashore near Charleston on July 14, taking seven lives and leaving $100,000 worth of damage in its wake. A tropical depression made landfall at Little River, South Carolina, near the North Carolina border on September 6. The last storm of the season to impact South Carolina reached hurricane strength before blowing by North Island on November 18. That was the last rain Eli had seen. It would take another tempest to break the drought.

North Island was particularly vulnerable. Located overlooking the shipping channels at the entrance to Winyah Bay, it was also the perfect location for a lighthouse. Furious winds slammed North Island frequently, often unexpectedly and with great force. Shrimpers and ship pilots feared them, for they made the shoal-riddled entrance to Winyah Bay even more treacherous to cross. The jetties made passage into Winyah Bay much safer. The lighthouse served as a guide and guardian of the channel. Eli stored his skiff under the keeper's house secured to one of the heart pine logs that held the house off the sandy ground.

He surveyed his garden. Everything needed water. In another day or so, unless the rains came, he would have to make the trek with the Nubians back to the freshwater pond up the island. He did not look forward to that.

He dipped a bucket into the cistern and whistled for the dog and the goats. They each drank a ration but not their fill. The Nubians were herded into the pen for the night. The flock of guinea hens found their perch in the live oak. Eli looked to the top of the tall pine tree. The osprey was finishing her supper.

He climbed the stairs of the lighthouse for evening prayers. Before striking an official match to light the twin-wick lamp, he marveled at the star-filled sky. Here on North Island, the stars did just what the Psalmist wrote, they declared the glory of God.

To the north, just above the forest, he saw the constellation known as Ursa Major, big bear. The familiar configuration of stars reminded him of the nights he spent fishing with his father and grandfather on the Black Sea. He remembered that seamen used the stars to navigate, using the big bear to locate the pole star.

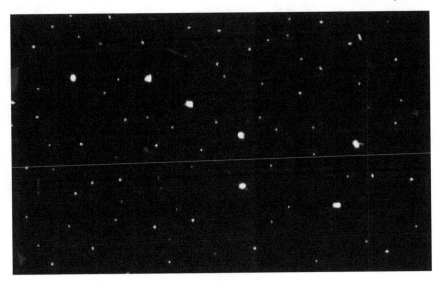

After a few moments of reflection, Eli once again lit the double-wicked lamp in the lens, sending a beam of light sweeping across the night sky.

He and the dog returned to the house. Remembering the sizeable human footprint near the garden, Eli locked the door, something he almost never did. The man and his dog enjoyed bluefish grilled in goat butter. He lit the three candles in the menorah and offered the usual prayer.

Eli had planned to go into Georgetown on Tuesday, December 26, because Meade's store would be closed on Monday, the day Christians called Christmas. The foreshadowing prophet wave caused him to rethink the plan. If there was an impending storm, he should make the trip sooner. Going to Georgetown required a full day, even in the best conditions. Now with the days short, it would be nearly a dawn-to-dusk journey. He decided to go on Friday, tomorrow, December 22.

As he drifted off to sleep, he remembered the muddy corset he had discovered. It must have belonged to a very large woman. He wondered about the enormous bare footprint he found near the wilting garden. He imagined a Goliath of a man looming somewhere further up North Island.

Or maybe the print was made by the same ample lady who lost her corset.

Or maybe there were two big people, a man and a woman.

With so much on his mind, his sleep was more fitful than usual. But he did sleep, and he dreamed of giants.

Chapter Twelve

Professor Rosen:

Every lighthouse within the purview of the United States Lighthouse Service was subject to inspection every three months. Those regular inspections included an examination of the daily logbook, a survey of all federal property, a determination of compliance with *The Pink Book* by the lighthouse keeper, and replenishing the supplies at the light station, especially the oil to keep the light burning.

Officer Roy Holden was a demanding and harsh inspector. Eli Solomon dreaded his quarterly visits.

Friday, December 22, 1916

Early Friday morning, well before dawn, Eli was awakened by his recurring nightmare. He rolled out of his hammock and went straight to the pickle jar, now nearly full. He hurried through the morning routine because he had to catch the incoming tide to make the thirteen-mile trip into Georgetown.

From the top of the lighthouse, he saw the sunrise. He said his usual prayers. Then he extinguished the wicks and cleaned the lamp and the lens much earlier than usual.

As he completed those tasks, he was startled to see the lighthouse tender at the dock. He saw a few crew members moving around on deck unloading supplies.

Officer Holden has come early, he thought. *I'll never get to Georgetown today.*

Eli descended the tower stairs and stored his cleaning supplies. He noticed the burlap bag. It was too late to dispose of it, so he hid it in the corner of the fuel shed, hoping it wouldn't be noticed.

He and the dog had not yet had breakfast, but that would have to wait. He opened the gate to the goat pen. Melchizedek, confused by the break in routine, took the goats out to the dunes to graze. Eli turned toward the keeper's house.

Roy Holden was sitting on the porch. Much to Eli's dismay, Officer Holden held the open pickle jar in his hand.

"Solomon, did you make this?"

Eli paused, "Yes sir, I did," speaking in broken English with a Ukrainian accent.

"It smells like piss. I'll bet it teste even worse!"

Stunned, Eli did not reply.

"I should have known a kike wouldn't know how to make liquor. Let's get this inspection done so I can find some decent whiskey."

Holden stood up and poured the contents of the jar out onto the sand.

Roy Holden was a stout man. His blond hair poked around the edges of his cap. He was short, and his thick neck disappeared into his broad shoulders. Blond eyebrows arched above steel-blue eyes. A thin blond mustache hovered above a small mouth. His uniform was crisp and white even in the hot December sun.

"I've already looked in the house. I can't believe you sleep in that damn hammock. I was hoping for a cup of coffee, but your stove was cold," he scorned, spitting in the sand. "Let's make this quick. Show me the log."

"Yes, sir." Eli went into the house and took the worn logbook from the shelf. Back on the porch, he handed the book to the inspector.

Roy Holden thumbed through the pages. "Solomon, you've got a weird handwriting. Some of your letters look like hieroglyphics. Do you record something every day?"

"Yes, sir."

"I see here that you've painted just about everything on the property."

"Almost everything. I request a new paintbrush and a new stipple brush, please."

"I see you've spent half a day picking up trash."

"Yes, sir."

"Is there that much trash in this godforsaken place?"

Eli had never thought of North Island as forsaken by God. He thought of his home as a sanctuary, a holy place.

"What'd you do with your trash, Solomon?"

Eli paused. He thought of the burlap bag containing the corset hidden in the fuel shed. "I take the trash into Georgetown to discard it."

"Let's look around the place."

At the dock, Holden ordered the crew to unload the lantern oil into the fuel shed. He gave orders to others to put the other supplies onto the porch of the keeper's house.

"You men, be quick. I want to get to Georgetown before noon."

Officer Roy Holden put on his white gloves and accompanied Eli up the tower. He rubbed his fingers across the newly cleaned Fresnel lens. Then he fingered the polished lamp and the mechanical works that turned the light. He found only traces of grime, but that was enough to draw criticism.

All things considered, the unexpected visit by the tender ship from the Lighthouse Service was going well. That was until Officer Holden inspected the fuel shed. The inspector noted the stacked cases of oil. Each case had four five-gallon containers; each can was marked with the distinctive Texaco star.

Then Roy Holden spotted the burlap bag. "Solomon, what is that? That burlap is nothing but a damn fire starter for all of this fuel. Get that out of here."

Eli knew he had made a serious mistake as he reached for the bag. Holden seized it before Eli could pick it up. "What's in here?"

Holden dumped the contents of the burlap bag on the ground. Out tumbled cans and bottles gathered from the shoreline and out came damp newspaper pieces and then the muddy corset.

"What the hell!" he bellowed.

When Roy Holden saw the corset, his face turned bright red. His scowl was harsh and severe. His voice loud, "You damn kike. Where'd you find that?"

Eli blurted out, "It was stuck in the mud on the bay side."

Roy Holden picked up the undergarment. He brushed away the dried mud revealing the initials, R.H., sewn in black thread. He looked around. No one else was near. He and Solomon stared at each other.

"Just who have you told about your secret discovery?"

"No one, sir."

"You best keep it that way. I swear I'll kill you if I ever hear that you have breathed one word about this. I ought to kill you just for finding it."

Eli was astonished by the inspector's intense, angry reaction. Completely bewildered, the lighthouse keeper said nothing.

After a long pause, Holden stuffed the corset back in the burlap bag. "Pick up this other trash, Solomon. I'm on my way to Georgetown. I'll take your garbage for you this time."

Still thoroughly confused, Eli did as he was told. Down on his hands and knees, gathering the trash, he knew he should have found a better place to keep the burlap bag. He struggled to understand the strong rage Officer Holden had in reaction to discovering the lady's garment. It seemed extreme, far out of proportion. After all, it was just trash, found in the mud.

Eli retrieved the two worn paintbrushes from the storage area and followed Holden.

Inspector Holden hurried back to the lighthouse tender ship. Along the way, he picked up a rock the size of his hand, a stone displaced from the jetty, and dropped it into the burlap bag.

In the ship's cabin, he found a pad of inspection forms. He checked none of the blocks but wrote in large letters across the page,

FAILED INSPECTION – FIRE HAZARD IN FUEL SHED.

He handed the report to the lighthouse keeper and muttered under his breath, "Remember, not one damn word."

Eli was hesitant but said, "Sir, about the paintbrushes?"

Holden looked at the worn and tattered brushes. He discarded the useless stipple brush into the burlap bag.

"Get me a pair of shears," he barked. A crew member handed him a large pair of scissors.

Holden took the paintbrush and trimmed the bristles back to less than an inch. He handed it to Eli, "There's your new stipple brush," he said. "Don't abuse it like the one I just threw away. And keep your damn mouth shut. I'll be back, Solomon."

Eli did not bother to ask again about removing the large loblolly pine next to the fuel shed. It wasn't a good time to ask about anything else.

Holden turned toward the wheel of the tender boat. "Push off," he shouted.   From the bridge of the *USLHS Cypress*, he gave the lighthouse keeper one last menacing glance.

Eli Solomon watched as the steam-powered tender moved toward Georgetown. The outflowing tide would make little difference to the *Cypress*, but for Eli, the trip to Georgetown would have to be postponed another day. In June, when the days are longer, he might have considered going. But now, in the abbreviated daylight hours of December, and with the tide going out, there was no way to make the trip today.

The lighthouse keeper knew that a storm was brewing somewhere out in the Atlantic, and there was a storm brewing in Roy Holden's soul. The prophet wave had given fair warning of the tempest at sea. Officer Holden's reaction to the undergarment was also a warning. But, why so strong? Eli expected criticism. That was part of every inspection. But Officer Holden's outburst seemed overblown. And, what did the initials R.H. mean? And, then it dawned on Eli, R.H. were the initials of the lighthouse inspector, Roy Holden. Could it be that inspector Holden had a wife also with the initials R.H.? He had never heard the man mention a wife. In fact, Eli recalled Officer Holden saying that he was not married.

After a few moments, Eli reasoned, *There was something about that corset that struck a nerve, something the inspector did not want anyone else to know.*

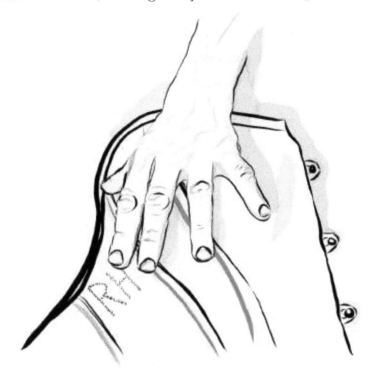

Eli needed to make a trip to Georgetown. It would have to be tomorrow, on Saturday. He could not wait another day. The trip would have to be made on *Shabbes*. It was against every teaching he held dear in his Jewish faith, but he had no other option.

Eli walked to the keeper's house. The supplies were stacked on the porch. They needed to be put away, and he and Melchizedek had not had breakfast.

The allowance of 200 pounds of pork was always less for Eli. As an observant Jew he did not eat the flesh of swine. Roy Holden kept most of it for himself. Eli usually divided his portion with the dog and with Samuel. In fact, Samuel had brought the goats in payment for the pork, though Eli did not expect reciprocation of any kind. He whistled for the dog who came loping over the dunes. The man tossed a chunk of the salted meat to his faithful companion.

Eli rolled the barrel of flour into the kitchen. He stored twenty-five pounds of rice, ten gallons of beans, fifty pounds of sugar, and twenty-four pounds of coffee on the high shelf. The four bushels of potatoes, the bushel of onions, the bushel of shelled corn, and four gallons of vinegar went on a lower shelf. One hundred pounds of dried beef was put away as well, but not until Eli had sliced off a piece for his very late breakfast.

As difficult as Officer Roy Holden was, Eli was glad to receive his allotment of supplies. With these provisions, along with the goats and the guineas, he fared very well on North Island. As he sat and enjoyed his beef, he wondered why Holden had become so upset when he saw the corset. He understood the inspector's point about the fire hazard. Maybe he deserved to fail the inspection. But Holden's reaction was so intense, like finding the undergarment was something personal.

Then Eli remembered again catching a glimpse of the initials sewn into the garment with black thread. He was sure they were R.H. His mind was spinning.

Could the initials stand for Roy Holden? Could the corset belong to Officer Holden? It was a large garment, large enough to fit the inspector. But why? How?

Eli tried to reconstruct the confusing conversation.

Holden had said, "I swear I'll kill you if I ever hear that you have breathed one word about this. I ought to kill you just for finding it." And then, again, "Remember, not one word."

Then the pieces fell into place in Eli Solomon's mind. He had heard of such, of men dressing as women. But, to his knowledge, he had never known anyone who actually did that. According to Jewish teaching, it would be considered an abomination.

Officer Holden had a distinguished career in the United States Coast Guard and now a position in the United States Lighthouse Service. If word ever got out that he was engaging in such behavior, his career and his name would be ruined. His fear was understandable.

Now he must be terrified that his secret will be known, and he will be disgraced.

Eli felt a surge of compassion for Roy Holden.

No wonder he's so fearful. He feels terribly alone.

Now somewhere faint in his memory Eli was almost certain that Officer Holden had told him that he didn't have a wife or children. As far as Eli knew, except for the crew of the *Cypress,* Holden was alone.

Eli understood what it was like to be alone, but for him, there was a difference between being alone and being lonely. Though he missed his wife and daughter even after all these years, he had never been as desperate as he imagined Roy Holden to be.

Eli finished his beef and offered a prayer of gratitude for the provisions of the day. To that, he added a prayer for Officer Holden.

With extra time in the afternoon ahead, he decided to take the goats back to the freshwater pond to slake their thirst.

Out in the deep-water channel of Winyah Bay, Roy Holden relinquished the wheel to the first mate. Below deck in his quarters, he pulled a coil of twine and a whiskey bottle from an overhead storage bin. He wrapped several loops of twine around the neck of the burlap bag, tying it securely. He opened the whiskey bottle and took a morning swig.

He climbed to the deck on the starboard side and lowered the burlap bag into the water, disposing of the trash collected by Eli Solomon.

Back in his quarters, Roy Holden drank and wondered.

Was Eli Solomon smart enough to figure out that the corset belonged to the inspector? Had he seen the initials?

The more he drank, the more he decided that he couldn't take a chance. He would have to dispose of the lighthouse keeper just as he had disposed of Solomon's trash.

Chapter Thirteen

Professor Rosen:

At the time of our story, steam-powered boats were relatively new, especially in Georgetown. Tall ships under sail were the primary way of transporting indigo and rice from Georgetown harbor. Even in 1916, those tall sailing ships carried most of the lumber from Atlantic Coast Lumber Company north and then, brought other supplies back into Georgetown.

Heiman Kaminski owned the Pee Dee Steamboat Company. He was the agent for the Clyde Line, featuring nine steam-powered passenger ships, all named for Native American tribes – *Apache, Mohawk, Lenape, Huron, Comanche, Arapahoe, Algonquin, Iroquois,* and *Cherokee*. Another of the Clyde ships was for freight only, the *Chippewa*. They usually traveled the coast from New York to Wilmington to Georgetown to Charleston to Jacksonville and back. Occasionally, one of the larger boats would go to the Caribbean Islands. One or more of the Clyde ships came in or out of Georgetown harbor nearly every day.

Toward the end of the rice days, several plantations had small steam vessels. There were several privately owned steam yachts on Winyah Bay. Mr. Edwin Kaminski had owned two. *The Rosa K* burned a few years back, and *The Palmetto* sank just off the Georgetown wharf in the July hurricane.

But the lighthouse tender was different. It was a smaller boat, making it more maneuverable. It had a double mast on both the bow and the stern with the single stack midship. The *Cypress* was powered by an oil-fired boiler that turned the steam-powered screw propeller. Back when the tender boats were completely under sail, the crew size was well over fifty sailors and officers. These smaller coastal ships powered by steam had one officer, the pilot, and a crew of a few men. Inspector Roy Holden was with the United Lighthouse Service and the captain of the lighthouse tender ship, *Cypress*.

Among the slaves of All Saints Parish, a favorite pastime was telling trickster stories. This form of folklore had origins in West Africa. Usually, these were animal tales in which smaller weaker creatures used their wits to outsmart the bigger and more powerful adversaries through superior cunning. The animals took on human traits, and the stories were told to teach important lessons about human behavior. On the Waccamaw rice plantations a favorite hero was Buh Rabbit. A favorite villain was Buh Bear. In many trickster stories, Buh Rabbit represented the slave, and Buh Bear represented the master.

Friday, December 22, 1916, continued

Early Friday morning, well before first light, Samuel Pringle limped down the steps of his shanty onto the path toward the cypress dock on the Sampit River. Along the way, he paused to light his pipe.

He glanced at the home of Maggie Howard across the sandy track. She was in the kitchen fixing breakfast. Samuel watched her move from the woodstove to the table as if she were gliding. He imagined being in her house, being at her table, being in her presence. He paused briefly to take a deep draw on the corncob pipe, then dismissing the impossible dream of Maggie from his mind, moved down the sandy path to his boat.

He rowed quietly down the Sampit toward the breaking dawn. The sky was filled with stars. There was no moon in view. High in the sky to the north, Samuel saw in the stars the shape known by the slaves of All Saints as the drinking gourd. Seven bright stars pointed the way north. Slaves that ran away from the plantation were told to follow the drinking gourd. Samuel had heard those stars also called the big bear, but he couldn't make out a bear at all.

Now, the eastern sky brightened. The horizon was streaked with wispy clouds of orange and pink ahead of the sunrise to come. Again, today, Samuel knew those clouds would burn away, but they held a faint promise of rain, maybe by Christmas.

The banks along the river were dark. Though the night air was cool, it was not the way December was supposed to feel. Samuel heard an animal stirring in the dark undergrowth, maybe a deer, a raccoon, a possum, or a skunk. A squawking blue jay roused her neighbors.

Friday 'spose to be de day jay bird totes sticks to stoke the fires of hell. Hit already felt hot 'nough. In the branches of a live oak draped in Spanish moss, squirrels scurried and chattered. A screech owl gave her last calls to the night shift. The Lowcountry was waking up to another unseasonably hot December day.

When Samuel arrived at the dock behind Meade's General Store, the backdoor was locked.

Mr. Meade runnin' late, he thought.

Using his walking stick, Samuel hobbled through the alley beside the jewelry store out to Front Street. Jasper already had his delivery wagon parked in front of the store loaded with an enormous cedar tree.

"Oonuh up wit da hens," said Samuel.

"Ain't no lazy chickens," said Jasper.

"Big cedar," commented the older man.

"Yep, took her from de swamp at first light," answered the mulatto boy.

With his gnarled fingers, Samuel stripped a few cedar needles from a low branch and smelled the aroma.

"Mr. Samuel, I brung dis," said Jasper holding up a small piece of jasmine vine with yellow blooms.

"A jasmine wit' flowers in winter time. I ain't neber seen nothing like it."

"How t'ings in da swamp dis mornin'?"

"Stirred up, Mr. Samuel. All confused like. Ain't neber seen nothin' like it. Cooters climbin' up logs in the sun like t'was June. Snakes still crawlin' and swimmin' like t'was July. Fish jumpin' up outta' da wata' like t'was August. And dem gators, Lawd, dem gators be as confused as me, eatin' ebert'ing in sight. I ain't neber seen not'in' like it. Summertime in December. I ain't goin' back for no more trees this year."

"Been 'round a heap more years dan oonah, but I ain't seen one like dis 'fo now."

"Granny say dis be de end times."

"Wait and see," said Samuel.

Richard Meade came down Front Street. "Yo' granny might be right, boy. It might be the end times when a high yella' keeps his word."

Meade looked at the large tree. "What did you say? A dime a foot?"

"No, suh. Two bits a foot."

"Dollar and a half for a cut-down tree?"

'No, suh. Two dollars and a half."

Richard Meade took two one-dollar bills from his wallet and handed them to Jasper.

"That should be plenty for this damn tree."

"No, suh, fi'ty cent more."

Meade fished in his pockets for two quarters and handed them to the young teamster. "You drive a hard bargain for a mulatto."

"Deal's a deal," said Jasper.

"Follow me to my house and help me get this tree set up. My wife is planning to decorate it today."

"Yes, suh."

Richard Meade walked to his home three blocks from the store. Jasper followed in the wagon and helped Meade mount the big cedar to a large wooden stand with a long lag bolt. The steel bolt twisting into the tree trunk released the fragrant cedar sap. Inside the house, the cedar filled the foyer with its size and with its aroma.

"Ain't she a beauty." said Jasper.

"It'll do," said Meade reluctantly. "I still think you charged too much."

Jasper didn't argue. He had the money. Meade had the tree. The deal was concluded. Most all of his people knew they couldn't do business with Richard Meade. That's why they did most of their shopping at Mr. Kaminski's Store.

It was late morning when Samuel limped to the back of the store to relieve himself in the river. As he did, he noticed an orange and black butterfly resting on top of a piling. He had seen many of these tiny creatures flying through Georgetown in October and November, but December was unusually late in the year to see one of them. He wiped his face and head with the faded red bandana.

Samuel saw an unusual boat anchored near Goat Island in Georgetown Harbor. It was the steam-powered tender, the *USLHS Cypress* of the U.S. Lighthouse Service.

Samuel had seen many other steam-powered vessels in Winyah Bay. The first was what was left of the *USS Harvest Moon*, a Union ship sunk during the Civil War by Confederate divers using a homemade torpedo. The smokestacks of the Yankee vessel were still visible at the south end of Mohawk Island at low tide.

Officer Roy Holden was the pilot of the *USLHS Cypress*. His job was to inspect lighthouses up and down the southeast Atlantic coast and to resupply the lighthouse stations. He was a hard man and a hard drinker. The combination made him downright unpleasant.

Dat man as mean as a wata' moccasin, thought Samuel.

The dinghy from the *Cypress* was moored at the dock behind the store near his own haint blue boat. Samuel noticed two hastily abandoned oars and an empty whiskey bottle in the dinghy.

If'n Cap'n Holden come to Georgetown in de middle of the day, dat can't be good, 'specially if'n he already be drinkin' whiskey. Can't be good.

Samuel could hear Roy Holden talking to Richard Meade in a loud voice. Back in the store he saw Holden with a brown bag in his left hand waving his right hand as he spoke. Holden was drunk.

"I need a shotgun." the inspector shouted. His speech was slurred.

Meade hesitated. "Don't you have a service revolver? Do you really need a shotgun on the ship?"

"Meade, get me a shotgun."

"I don't know, Roy. You're not in very good shape to go hunting.

171

"Damn it to hell, I want to buy a shotgun." he demanded.

Meade was hesitant, but he needed all the business he could muster.

"I have two, both made by Remington, a .16 gauge and a .12 gauge," said Meade, still reluctant but removing both guns from a locked case behind the counter. "If you are hunting ducks or quail, the .16 gauge is plenty. If you are after something bigger, like a deer, you need the .12 gauge."

"I'm hunting something big with a damn big mouth. Give me that .12 gauge and a box of shells," Holden demanded.

Meade placed the Model 1910 .12 gauge side-by-side Remington on the counter and a box of shells. "This is a new shotgun, but Remington discontinued making this Model 1910 several years ago."

"It'll do what I need it for. Put it on the Lighthouse Service account."

"Is this for lighthouse business?"

"It sure as hell is." Holden staggered.

Samuel grabbed a chair. "Have a seat, suh."

Holden sat and signed the bill for the double-barrel shotgun.

Meade asked, "Roy, where's your crew?

"Hell, I don't know. Drinking, looking for whores, how the hell do I know? I gave them the rest of the day off. Told'em we'd weigh anchor at first light tomorrow. I've got some private business to tend to."

Holden rested the shotgun on his lap, opened the brown bag, broke the seal on the bottle inside, and took a long drink.

Samuel realized that his friend Eli Solomon was in danger. Everyone was silent for a moment. Then, Samuel Pringle told this story in his flowing Gullah accent.

> Once upon a time, a long time ago, 'twasn't oonuh time, 'twasn't my time, Buh Bear was makin' life miserable for Buh Rabbit. Buh Bear was tauntin' and teasin' and generally doin' e'erythin' he could to pester Buh Rabbit.

> Buh Rabbit had enough of it and hatched a plan. Early one mornin' 'bout daylight, Buh Rabbit went down to de riber to discuss dis 'dicament with Buh Gator and Buh Cooter. Neither one had been able to bask in de sunshine so dey was still sluggish and slow. He made an 'greement to bring a tasty meal of bear meat fo' de gator and de cooters to share. He told dem jest what to do.

> Late dat afternoon, Buh Bear caught up with Buh Rabbit. He started in on him with his pesterin' ways. Buh Rabbit said, "Buh Bear, dis has surely been a hot sultry day. I'm going down to de riber to walk on de watta'."

> Buh Bear said, "Buh Rabbit, oonuh can't walk on de watta'. Only de Lawd can do dat."

> "Yes, I can," said Buh Rabbit, kinda smart alecky like. "Follow me. I'll show oonuh how 'tis done."

> Buh Rabbit led Buh Bear down to de riberbank. Buh Cooter and his friends were floatin' just below de surface of de watta'. Buh Rabbit step out on de watta' and walk across de shells of dem cooters.

"Try, Buh Bear. 'T will cool oonuh off."

Buh Bear stuck his toes in de watta'. He knowd he couldn't walk on de watta'. Just den he saw a big log floatin' in de riber. Not to be outdone, he stepped on de log.

"Look at me, Buh Rabbit. I'm walkin' on de watta'."

But 'twasn't a log he be standin' on. 'twas de back of Buh Gator. Buh Gator took Buh Bear out to de middle of de riber. He roll over dumpin' Buh Bear into de deep watta'. Den Buh Gator grab 'em in dem big jaws and et 'em up. Dere was plenty of leftovers fo' all of de cooters in de riber.

Samuel Pringle wiped the sweat from his face and head. He looked Roy Holden in the eye.

"Nigga', what are you looking at?"

"Look at oonuh. Dem dat torments, git dey comeuppance."

Roy Holden's face flushed bright red. "Meade, you got an uppity nigga' there. You best do something about him. I've got to deal with an uppity kike."

With that, Holden stumbled out of the backdoor of the store to the waiting dinghy. He was so drunk that he couldn't steady himself enough to get in the boat.

"Nigga', hold this shotgun."

Samuel did as he was told. Holden sat down in the dinghy, oars in place, and the bottle between his knees.

"Hand me that discontinued Remington. I'm gonna' discontinue a stupid, nosey kike before sundown."

As he rowed away from the dock down the Sampit River toward Winyah Bay, his stroke was remarkably strong. With the outgoing tide, he would reach the lighthouse well before sundown.

Richard Meade shouted, "Get back in here, nigga'. What do you mean, telling that fool story to Officer Holden?"

Samuel thought a moment before speaking, "Dem dat torments git dey comeuppance."

He stared at Meade. He saw the fear in his bulging eyes, always the fear, in Meade and in Holden, too.

"What are you staring at, nigga'"

"If'n de shoe fit, wear hit."

"By damn, you are an uppity nigga'. I ought to shoot you."

Samuel turned and walked to the front of the store. He kept busy and quiet the rest of the day. Meade waited on customers with his usual cheerful way encouraging them to spend money, but Meade and Samuel didn't speak to each other the rest of the day.

At the end of the day, Samuel lowered himself into the blue boat and began rowing up the Sampit toward the Gullah Line.

He wondered what was happening out on North Island.

He remembered several times when he had looked down the double barrel of a shotgun. It was a frightening feeling. He did not want his friend Eli to have a weapon pointed at him. There wasn't much he could do to help Eli, but in the few moments he had the shotgun in his hand, he made sure the safety was locked.

Chapter Fourteen

Professor Rosen:

The traditions of Hanukkah are not without violence. The attack on Jerusalem by the Maccabees in 165 B.C.E. is a clear example.

Another Hanukkah tradition is the eating of dairy products, especially cheese. This is done in memory of the Jewish heroine Judith, whose story is difficult to date but perhaps goes back to a time before Nebuchadnezzar reigned in Babylon. According to legend, Judith saved her village from Assyrian attackers. Judith fed wine and cheese to the Assyrian General Holofernes until he became so drunk that he fell into a drunken stupor. Judith seized his sword and cut off his head, saving her village from Assyrian atrocities.

This dramatic and gruesome scene from the Apocrypha has been depicted many times in works of art by Caravaggio, by Goya, and by Michelangelo on the ceiling of the Sistine Chapel, just to name a few.

By setting Hanukkah on the 25th of the Hebrew lunar month of Kislev, the Jews made sure that the nights would be dark. By setting it in Kislev, they made sure the day would be very short and the sun very dim.

If we see Hanukkah as intentionally, not accidentally, placed at the moment of the darkest sun and darkest moon, then one aspect of the candles seems to be an assertion of our hope for renewed light.

Roy Holden was a man living a double life. The darkness of the season was mirrored in the darkness of Roy Holden's soul.

Friday, December 22, 1916, continued

Officer Roy Holden was a seaman. Even drunk as he was, he rowed the dinghy from the *Cypress* with ease, still holding a true course. The tide was moving out to sea, and Holden caught the current. He rowed a few strokes and took a drink, rowed a few more, and swigged again. It was a rhythm he maintained throughout the hot afternoon. The sun was high in the cloudless sky as he passed Frazier Point. There was little breeze. After less than an hour, his shirt was soaked, and his tattooed forearms glistened with sweat.

Along his route, a bottle-nosed dolphin arched in his wake, but Holden was too busy with his own bottle to notice. Here and there an alligator in search of a meal slithered from the bank, but Holden's mind was on his own prey. He was convinced that the lighthouse keeper knew his secret, one he could not trust to anyone except his closest consorts. He looked at the shotgun and the box of shells in the stern of the dinghy. By sundown, the problem would be solved. The lighthouse keeper would be missing. A report would be filed, and soon, a replacement would be found.

When Officer Roy Holden arrived at the North Island Light, he did not bother to moor the small boat at the dock. He pulled it part way out of the water, the bow resting on the sand. He drained the whiskey bottle and tossed it into the bay. Looking around, he saw nothing moving. A lone crow in the top of a loblolly announced his arrival on the island. Then the guinea fowl began to make a ruckus. As Holden picked up the shotgun, the guineas scattered, some under the house, some to the live oak. The inspector loaded both barrels. He put a handful of extra shells in his pocket.

He staggered to the house. He stumbled up the stairs. No one was at home. The guineas were still making a racket. The goats were not in their pen. He checked the tower. No sign of activity. He looked toward the jetties and saw only the constant waves pounding the coast, the tide moving out to sea.

Then, above the squawking of the crow and the guineas, he heard a slight sound coming from the woods. It was the sound of bells, goat bells, drifting from further up the island. Cautiously, the unsteady inspector moved past the drought-damaged garden and plodded awkwardly up the sandy path into the thick woods.

He moved slowly, deliberately. *This is like the Panama jungle*, he thought.

Further along, he heard the bells more distinctly. Eli Solomon had taken his goats to drink. Roy Holden had never before been to the interior of North Island, but he had heard about the freshwater pond.

I could use a little fresh water myself, he thought.

As the inspector moved along the uneven path, he kept the shotgun at the ready. He intended to kill the lighthouse keeper the moment he saw him. Through the cabbage palms and the palmettos, beneath the live oaks with their curtains of Spanish moss, he stalked.

His boot stepped on a dry pine stick. The breaking stick made a cracking sound.

The dog, drinking water, heard the sound and turned his head facing the trail. His eyes and ears were alert, but he did not bark.

The goats, having had their fill of water, fidgeted, ringing their bells more clearly.

Eli, ever attentive to the behavior of his animals, knew that someone was approaching. Quietly he moved closer to a large live oak. The dog gave a low growl.

On the opposite bank, three big alligators were basking in the afternoon sun.

Out of the shadows emerged the figure of a drunken Officer Roy Holden, red-eyed and stumbling, with the shotgun pointed straight at Eli.

"I told you I'd be back, you son of a bitch. You leave me no choice but to kill you. Say your Hebrew prayers, kike."

Melchizedek barked loudly.

Roy Holden shouldered the shotgun and pulled the trigger on the first barrel, but the gun did not fire. He fumbled with the gun and tried the second barrel, but no shot was fired.

"Damn!" he yelled, taking the safety off of both barrels. He turned to fire at the lighthouse keeper, but Eli slipped behind the live oak. The dog leapt at Holden knocking him off balance before the gun could discharge.

The commotion sent the smallest alligator sliding into the dark water.

Drunk as he was, Holden regained his footing and turned to fire at the dog, but out of the corner of his eye he caught a horrifying specter – the same ghostly figure that had seen him on the beach two weeks earlier – the ebony man with cotton hair and beard. The man rose from behind a cabbage palm across the pond. Holden aimed directly at the apparition, but too late.

Holden tried to fire, but the growling dog bared his teeth and leapt again before he could get a shot off. This time the dog's teeth gashed Holden's right arm above the elbow to the artery. The dislodged, discontinued Remington splashed into the water sinking, unfired, into the mire.

The two largest alligators scrambled toward the safety of the pond, their cold-blooded bodies warmed by the hot December sun and now thoroughly agitated.

Holden floundered on the sandy bank, clutching at his right arm. It was spurting a steady stream of blood. The dog charged him again and, with a mighty leap, knocked him backwards into the pond. The two largest alligators glided toward him through the dark water. The third alligator came to the surface.

Usually light feeders in the winter, the alligators were hungry. Their metabolism was raised from the warm December sun. Now, they were ready to eat. And, there was blood in the water. There was plenty of blood. The dark water was stained crimson by the blood gushing from Holden's arm.

The big reptiles were provoked, ready to attack, and attack they did. Roy Holden's last words were unintelligible screams drowned out by gurgling. Thrashing the water in their typical death rolls, the gators dismembered the dying man.

The dog moved close to Eli, licking tears from his face. As his sobbing subsided, Eli became aware of a hand on his shoulder. On this remote island, Eli could not imagine who would be touching him. Slowly he turned his head. Through his blurred eyes, he saw the kind face of a Black man, the man behind the cabbage palms. His hair and beard were white. His face kind and compassionate. The man did not speak. He helped Eli to his feet and waved good-bye.

Back at the lighthouse, the goats went straight into their pen. They had plenty of water. And, they had more than enough excitement. Eli closed the gate. The guineas shuffled in the sandy yard as if nothing had happened.

Eli walked with Melchizedek, the dog who had saved his life, to the Winyah Bay side of the island expecting to find the lighthouse tender ship at the dock. The *Cypress* was not there. The crew was not there. In the distance, out beyond the jetties, the lighthouse keeper saw an empty dinghy carried by the tide, drifting far out into the Atlantic Ocean.

Guineas went about life as usual, pecking around the yard and the dunes searching for insects. Eli sat on the porch of the house, trying to make sense of the events of the day. In an odd way, he grieved for Roy Holden. He pondered how he would explain to the crew of the *Cypress* what had happened. How could he explain it to the Lighthouse Service? He had promised Roy Holden that he would not reveal his secret. He was determined to keep that promise. It seemed more important now than before.

Eli was weeping again, tears flowing slowly, rolling along his sideburns and into his beard. It had been one of the most difficult days of his entire time as a lighthouse keeper. Atlantic storms were manageable, but a drunken man with a shotgun was unpredictable.

Eli had witnessed horrible deaths, some in the pogroms, including the loss of his own wife and daughter. Every unnecessary death by violence is tragic, and the demise of Officer Roy Holden was among them.

Eli Solomon put his head in his hands and cried softly. The goats were safe in their pen. The guineas fussed as they ventured under the house looking for bugs. The dog came near to the despondent man, searching his sad face. Eli put his arm around the animal and wept. The dog held steady and again licked the tears from the man's cheeks.

When the lighthouse keeper had collected himself, he climbed the tower of North Island Light. He prayed as usual with a special prayer for Roy Holden. Sundown was the beginning of *Shabbes*. He had made the decision that he would have to go to Georgetown on Saturday, but he would go early enough to be at the synagogue for the *Shabbes* service. In doing so, he would have to violate several regulations of the Lighthouse Service.

The death of Roy Holden weighed heavy on his mind. Whom should he tell? Who would believe him? What would he say? Roy Holden had been a difficult person for Eli Solomon, but Eli realized that, for some reason, the lighthouse inspector was afraid. Eli had seen a side of Holden that perhaps others had not seen, but Holden did not think he could trust Eli with his dark secret.

Officer Holden's career with Lighthouse Service had been the core of his life. Eli did not want to destroy whatever good name Roy Holden might have. There was only one other witness, the strange Black man with the white hair, and he might have been a ghost as some suspected, but Eli knew he was a person of compassion. Of that, he was sure.

How could he report Holden's terrible death without defaming the inspector's name? Was there anyone he could trust with the truth of Roy Holden's death? Eli could think of only one – Samuel Pringle. He would have to decide whether to tell his Black friend or not.

Back in the keeper's house, Eli sat looking out the window as the sun faded. The shells along the windowsill, as beautiful as they were, reminded him that all life must come to an end. It had been so for his wife and his daughter, for his parents and grandparents, for his Uncle Mordecai. The shells were simply what had been left behind, the residue of death.

Then questions came to his mind. *What will be left behind when my life ends? Will I leave anything to be remembered, to be cherished by anyone? That will be for others to decide. Today, I will remember those that I have loved. And I will remember Officer Roy Holden. Like all people, he was a mixture of good and evil. I will hold to the good and preserve his memory.*

It was Friday, December 22. *Shabbes* began at sundown. It was the fourth night of Hanukkah, the 28 of Kislev, 5677. It was the night of the new moon and the winter solstice. It was the darkest day of the year. And yet, the Georgetown Light continued its circle overhead, eighteen miles out into the Atlantic, and back over Winyah Bay.

Chapter Fifteen

Professor Rosen:

The rice planters of All Saints Parish in the Georgetown area had a preference for slaves from equatorial West Africa. Those were the countries where rice was grown, and many of the adult slaves from that area were familiar with the methods of cultivating the crop. Not only was the land along the rivers flowing into Winyah Bay suitable for raising Carolina Gold, but the climate was also much the same as West Africa.

When the slaves came, they brought with them elements of their culture. While African tribes varied in cultural practices, they also had many things in common, among them indigenous religion. In all of those African cultures, religion was a part of every aspect of life. Along the Southeast coast of the United States, the slaves from various tribes developed a unique Gullah language. Many of their beliefs and burial practices came with them to the Sea Islands of South Carolina. So, too, did many of their traditional beliefs about the relationship between good and evil.

Belief in shamanism was prevalent among the slaves of All Saints Parish. On every plantation, there were conjurers or root doctors. A shaman could offer guidance or perform cures. Prescribing ointments, teas, and herbal remedies was common. Among the slaves, there were thought to be several kinds of malevolent spirits. A shaman could offer advice about how to avoid or destroy those spirits.

Because Samuel Pringle was a caulbearer, many thought he might have become a shaman. But Samuel was not as superstitious as many other Gullah people. He believed that all people were capable of both good and evil.

Friday, December 22, 1916, continued

Samuel Pringle picked up his hat from the nail at the backdoor, climbed into the blue boat, and in almost total darkness, rowed away from Richard Meade's store. It was the dark of the moon. Though the stars were bright, the night was much longer than the day.

Nearly 'bout winter, he thought to himself. *Sho' don't seem like hit.*

Samuel had been taught by the old folks to be careful in the dark. As he rowed through the still water, he remembered some of the old sayings:

If'n oonuh can't git hit done in de daylight hit probably ain't worth doin'. Folks who move around in de dark is usually up to no good.

A screech owl cried from a live oak near the bank. Squirrels rustled in the dry leaves along the ground. Samuel listened to the sounds around him and to the rhythm of his oars dipping in the dark Sampit.

Some of the old folks believed there were things to fear that lurked in the dark. In his boyhood days on the plantation, Samuel had heard stories about hags, women who could shed their skin, and move around in the night doing all kinds of mischief. Old man Jefferson, the oldest slave at Greenfield and a root doctor, told him long ago that if he ever saw a hag, he should find her skin and put salt on it so she couldn't put it back on by daylight. Old man Jefferson said that would get rid of a hag.

Though Samuel was a caulbearer and had the gift of second sight, as far as he knew, he had never seen a hag. In fact, he had known very few women he would have even suspected of being a hag.

Rachel told him before they stepped over the broom at Chicora, "Neber a woman sets out to be a hag. 'tis only a mean man dat make her so."

The evil plat-eyes were worse than hags. They were spirits that could change to other forms or shapes. Sometimes they looked like animals. At other times they took on grotesque features. They haunted low ground like swamps and old rice fields and especially cemeteries. They have front teeth, but no back teeth. When they are not disguised, they have one big eye, like a round plate. They come in the fog late at night, or before first light in early morning mist after a good rain.

The old folks said the plat-eyes were guarding buried treasure or the graves of the dead. Samuel had never seen a plat-eye. He had been around a lot of swamps and rice fields, but he made a habit of avoiding cemeteries, especially at night.

'T ain't much danger of a plat-eye tonight. We ain't had a hard rain, and dey ain't no treasure to be found.

Then he remembered the five-dollar gold piece given to him by Miz Pringle.

Best hide hit, he thought, *and de cigar, too.*

He stopped rowing for a moment allowing the boat to drift forward quietly in the water. The call of a night heron broke the silence. Samuel listened. His eyes adjusted to the darkness that was illuminated only by starlight. He saw a familiar shape moving on the far bank. A large buck moved through a thicket and disappeared. He thought to himself,

'Der ain't not'in' to be 'fraid of.

As he rowed again, his mind wandered to haints.

Haints were different from hags and plat-eyes, at least to Samuel. He did believe in them. They were restless spirits trapped between this world and the next. They couldn't get settled. A haint could take the form of a ghost or a person. Samuel had heard tell of a haint on Pawleys Island. He was known as the Gray Man. Some said he was the ghost of an old sea captain who showed up before each hurricane to give a warning.

Some said that out on North Island, there was a little girl who did the same. She was the child of a former lighthouse keeper. She had died clinging on her daddy's back during a hurricane and now came to warn others when a storm was coming.

Because he believed in haints he had painted the door frame on his house bright blue to keep them away. He had long ago painted his rowboat the same color because some thought the boat came from a ghost ship.

Haints don't neber hurt no body. Dey jest scares 'em real bad, thought Samuel. *Dey like hermit crabs tryin' to find a shell to rest in. Dey jest restless and keep other folks uneasy.*

The nice thing about haints was that, even though they were scary, they were also kind.

'Dey really don't mean no harm. 'Dey jest keeps on doin' de same thing on and on. If'n a haint rattles chains, he most always be a chain rattler.

Back in the old days, a conjure doctor, somebody like Old Man Jefferson, would make a boo-daddy from pluff mud, Spanish moss, and sweetgrass. The doll-like talisman might be decorated with bits of shells, bones, or feathers. Folks believed that boo-daddies could renew their power every month, under the full moon, by receiving a sip of nectar from a marsh oyster. Boo-daddies were crafted with large heads and shapeless bodies. They were thought to protect the owner from all evil spirits.

He could still hear the words of Old Man Jefferson, "If'n oonuh be scairt o' dem haints, hags, 'n plat-eyes what be roamin' roun' afta' dark, oonuh can keep a boo-daddy in yo' pocket or roun' yo' neck, and dem scaries be stayin' way from oonuh an' go mess wit' somebody whut ain't got no pertection. Dem scaries be runnin' an' stayin' gon' fo' good."

Samuel Pringle might have become a conjure doctor himself. He had the gift of second sight. The trouble was he didn't fully believe in the spirit world. He had lived a long time and had never known a hag, nor had he ever seen a plat-eye. He wasn't sure about haints but didn't take chances. He used the haint blue paint just in case a one might be about. From Samuel's point of view, there was plenty enough evil in the hearts of the folks you could see. He didn't need to believe in dark forces he couldn't see.

As the blue rowboat approached the cypress dock near Samuel's shanty, a thick gray cloud hung over the Gullah Line. It was not fog or mist; it was wood smoke. Rather than lighting his corncob pipe, he enjoyed the aroma of burning hardwood.

Folks cookin' supper, thought Samuel, his stomach growling, wondering what he would eat.

He followed the sandy path that led to his home. As he hobbled along using the cedar walking stick, he could see Maggie in her kitchen, busy with supper. John Howard had always bragged on Maggie's cooking.

Sho' would like to gits my feets under her table, he thought.

189

He climbed the steps to his door and entered his humble abode. With a few pieces of heart pine kindling and small oak logs, he started a fire in his cooking stove. Then he reheated the same pot of beans and rice he had eaten from the night before.

He went back out to his porch and sat down on the top step. He lit his corncob pipe and smoked and thought. Friday had been a long hard day. The combination of dealing with Richard Meade and Roy Holden was wearying. He wondered what had happened out on North Island. He could see the sweep of the Georgetown Light, so it seemed that Eli Solomon was unharmed.

The look in Holden's eye, the drunken glare, had frightened Samuel more than any haint. He worried about his friend Mr. Eli. He had little doubt that Officer Holden intended to shoot the lighthouse keeper. But why?

Though he had second sight, and Samuel could often see the darkness in a person's soul, he could not always discern the source of that darkness. More likely, it was the same kind of fear he saw every day in Richard Meade.

Taking a puff from his pipe, Samuel was glad that he at least had a chance to be sure the safety was on the shotgun before he handed it to Holden.

The angry red face of Richard Meade came to his mind. He knew Meade was afraid, and his hate grew from his fear. Was he afraid of Samuel because he was Black? Was Holden afraid of Mr. Eli because he was from someplace else?

Samuel thought to himself, *Bein' 'fraid troubles folks' soul and stirs up dey spirit. Fear's a bad thing fo' evuhbody.*

Back inside the shanty, Samuel ate the rest of the beans and rice from the pot. The warm food filled his belly and made him sleepy. He took off his boots and clothes and, as usual, said an evening prayer. He was soon sound asleep.

Sometime in the night, Samuel was awakened by a noise and a bright light coming from his yard. He slipped out of bed and crawled on his hands and knees to the window. Peering around the casement, he saw fire. The heart pine bench was ablaze. The flames illuminated four mounted figures, armed with torches, rifles, and shotguns. Each wore a white hood and rode a hooded horse.

Samuel ducked down below the window. Would they set his house on fire? Would they shoot him if he limped outside?

He waited, listening to his own breath, hearing the pounding of his own heart. He sat with his back against the door to offer some resistance to anyone who might try to enter. From that position, he could see the window reflected in the broken mirror on the wall above his bed. He watched and waited.

Then he heard footsteps coming up the seven stairs. Still, he waited, pressing his back against the door. A robed, hooded figure moved in front of the window. Samuel could see the white hood with cut-out eye holes. As the man peered into the window, Samuel could see the eyes. They were the same bulging eyes that he saw every day of the week. They were eyes crowned by a single eyebrow, eyes filled with hate, eyes filled with fear. Though nothing else about the person was recognizable, Samuel knew those eyes, and he knew the man behind them.

Samuel struggled to raise himself to his feet. He took a long deep breath, offered a quick prayer, and then quickly opened the door.

"Good evenin', Mr. Meade. Can I hep oonuh?"

The startled man raised a shotgun toward Samuel. Suddenly, reacting just as he had done with the ax handle a few days before, Samuel seized the double barrels of the weapon with his left hand wrenching it away from the hooded man. Samuel saw the other men raise their weapons.

"Mr. Meade, tell dem men to put dey guns down."

Meade did as he was told. The men slowly put their guns down.

"Ain't nobody be hurt here tonight," Samuel said.

Samuel broke the shotgun down and emptied the shells from both barrels. He handed the gun back to the man robed in white.

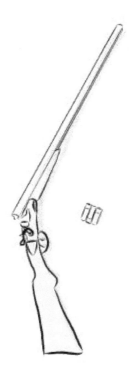

The frightened man in white scrambled down the steps into the yard, shocked that he had been recognized and confronted by a man he was used to harassing. The three other masked and robed Klansmen stared in disbelief at the Black man standing in the doorway of his shanty clad only in his underwear. They could not believe that he had the guts to tell their leader, Richard Meade, what to do, or that Richard Meade had relented and retreated. It was a complete reversal of what they expected to happen.

In the fading light from the burning bench, the would-be shooters saw the glistening black muscular arms, chest, and shoulders of a man past seventy years. His powerful form was enough to frighten anybody intending harm.

"Let's get outta' here," a voice familiar to Samuel shouted.

Samuel watched as the four hooded intruders mounted their horses and left in a hurry. He waited until they were out of sight. Samuel sat down on the top step of his home, trembling, watching as the embers of the bench burned low.

Across the way, a lantern was lighted in Maggie Howard's house. She came to her door wearing a thin cotton dress, so thin the light from the window behind her revealed her womanly shape. She came barefooted, running across the sandy track. At the bottom of Samuel's steps, she stopped.

Maggie looked into Samuel's face. She looked past the white flecks in his hair and his beard, past the wrinkles around his eyes, past the high cheekbones, past the tight lips. She looked into his deep moist black eyes.

Samuel looked at Maggie. He saw a woman who had suffered much but had remained strong, a woman both tough and tender. He looked into her soft eyes and reached out a hand to her.

She took his hand.

"Oonuh alright?"

"Jest fine. Sorry I ain't got no clothes on. Things happened quick-like."

Maggie came up and sat next to Samuel on the top step. She leaned against him, her head on his shoulder. He put a strong but gentle arm around her waist. A tear rolled down his cheek. They were touching for the first time, something they had both wanted for a long time.

"De might 'a kilt oonuh, might 'a burnt de house down. Don't want nothin' be done happened to oonuh."

"I'm alright. Best I be in years." He gently stroked her back. She held his arm across her breasts. They sat holding each other without words for a long while.

"'Preciate de Christmas tree."

"Welcome."

"Can oonuh eat Christmas supper wit us?"

Samuel's heart leapt in his chest. "Sho' can. Much obliged."

They sat there for a long while, neither one wanting the closeness to end. Finally, Maggie leaned up and kissed him on the cheek. "Oonuh take care."

Samuel didn't say anything. Another tear escaped his eye. He just watched as the beautiful Maggie walked barefooted back across the track, the light from her window shining through her thin cotton dress.

Samuel sat on his porch for a long time. The smoldering pine bench collapsed, causing the flames to flare up again. Samuel wanted to wait until the embers had died down completely before going back to sleep. He struggled to his feet, limping back into his shanty. He found the cigar and the gold coin and hid them in the small cupboard inside a sack of flour. He picked up his pipe, matches, and tobacco pouch and returned to the porch, still wearing only his underwear.

Smoking his pipe, he watched the last of the bench burn to ashes. Off to the east, he saw the beam of the North Island light sweeping across Winyah Bay.

Reckon Mr. Eli alright. He took comfort at the thought.

The shortest day of the year had been a long one for Samuel. Jasper's big tree cut from the Sampit Swamp, Roy Holden's rage, the shotgun,

195

and the whiskey, the four men with hoods and weapons burning his bench, the eyes and the voice that he was sure belonged to Richard Meade, and then Maggie came to him as if she were an angel sent by God.

The accident at the lumber mill had crippled him and robbed him of his manhood, and even though he couldn't be a husband to Rachel in every way, she had a way of touching him, speaking to him, that made him feel every bit a man.

Maggie Howard had done that for him tonight, sitting beside him on the porch. Maggie had awakened something in him he had not felt since Rachel. He imagined what she could do for him if they were lying together under her covers. He tried to push that pleasant thought out of his mind with a whispered prayer.

> Dear, Lawd, please look ober Maggie and her woman child.
> Please look ober Mr. Eli.
> Please, Lawd, help Mr. Meade get ober his hate.
> And bring his child home safe.
> Jesus' name, Amen.

The ashes of the bench were no longer glowing though smoke was still rising in the warm December air. The strong beam of the lighthouse circled the star-filled sky. He took one last draw on his pipe and knocked the ashes out. He cast one more glance at the place where there had been a bench. Through the thick smoke and the faint light from sparks rising from the dying embers, even the live oak tree had a ghostly appearance.

Gonna' build another bench. Gonna' paint hit haint blue.

Chapter Sixteen

Professor Rosen:

The Palmetto State had the reputation of being hospitable to newcomers. South Carolina was not started for religious reasons, as was the case with some of the other colonies. The eight Lord Proprietors were entrepreneurs. South Carolina was, from the beginning, a business proposition. For that reason, any person of any background who could make the colony more profitable was welcomed. The oldest city in the state, Charleston, was evidence that differing groups were accepted. The variety of churches and one of the oldest synagogues in the United States illustrated that diversity.

Georgetown was established on the Sampit River in 1729. By 1732, the city was an official port. The Jewish community had found a place of hospitality and opportunity in Georgetown.

To be an observant Jew requires prayer. Prayer is a part of everyday life. Some of our prayers are prescribed for regular times of worship on *Shabbes* and at festivals.

But prayer for an observant Jew is also spontaneous, a constant reminder of God's presence in our lives. Prayer is not something that happens only in the synagogue. Our first thought in the morning is a prayer thanking God for returning our souls to us.

There are prayers to be recited just before eating or lighting candles and prayers to recite before going to bed at night. Traditional Judaism has always stressed the importance of praying in Hebrew. The Talmud states that it is permissible to pray in any language that you can understand. Eli Solomon prayed in Hebrew for the memorized prayers and in Yiddish when his prayers were spontaneous.

Being a devout Jew means keeping Torah, but it also means attending to the moment. An observant Jew may offer a blessing upon witnessing lightning or a falling star, lofty mountains, or vast deserts, or the expanse of the ocean. A faithful Jew recites a blessing upon hearing thunder rumble through the heavens, and at the sight of a rainbow. Observant Jews are, most of all, attentive.

By keeping *Shabbes*, we help joy increase. By celebrating the holidays, we create community. By marking the events of human life, we deepen our capacity to care for each other. By being attentive to the beauty of creation, we become mindful of our responsibility to make this wounded world whole again. By being observant, we encourage healing, compassion, integrity, and love.

Eli Solomon lived an observant life every day in the solitude of North Island, but it was difficult to keep all of the lighthouse regulations and, at the same time, keep Jewish mitzvoth, that is, precepts and commandments. Eli was a conflicted man on both counts.

Saturday, December 23 (*Shabbes*)

After a quick breakfast, Eli offered a brief morning prayer, not from the lantern room atop the lighthouse, but from the keeper's house.

> It is good to thank You, O Lord,
> To sing praises to your exalted name
> To proclaim your love every morning
> And your faithfulness every night.

Eli left North Island in the skiff before 5:00 A.M. His mind was certain this was the right thing to do; his heart was a bundle of contradictions. It was *Shabbes*, but he had work to do, the hard work of rowing and sailing to Georgetown for supplies. He was acting contrary to the Lighthouse Service Pink Book, which instructed him to extinguish the wicks a half-hour after dawn and to clean and prepare the light before 10:00 A.M. On this day he would do neither. The light would just have to burn itself out when the fuel in the lamp was spent. At least on this day he didn't have to worry about being inspected, but Officer Roy Holden had never been more on his mind.

From a tree on the shore, an owl hooted, as if questioning the lighthouse keeper's violation of regulations. The beam from the lighthouse swept its circled path across Winyah Bay and back over the ocean as he pulled the oars through the water. After a few minutes the wind picked up. Eli lifted the mast, dropped the daggerboard, hoisted the sail, and fixed an oar on the stern. The canvas caught the wind and propelled the small boat into the current of the incoming tide.

At first light, the skiff passed Ballast Island, an island created at the place where British ships in colonial times had dumped ballast stones to enable their vessel to navigate the narrow channel through the bay.

A great blue heron stood on one leg, fishing in the shallows. As the sun climbed through the clouds, the whole sky turned red.

The boat glided past the exposed stacks of the *USS Harvest Moon*, a Union ship sunk at the south end of Mohawk Island during the Civil War. Under the cover of darkness, Confederate divers had delivered the homemade torpedo that took the ship down.

Though the lighthouse was out of sight beyond Cat Island, Eli saw the last sweep of the beam before the light went out. He knew the oil in the lamp was completely gone. He planned to make his first order of business cleaning and preparing the light when he returned at the end of the day.

His thoughts turned to the death of Roy Holden. He had seen alligators devour ducks, and he knew the reptiles were always a danger. But he had never imagined the violence he had seen on Friday afternoon. The alligators' behavior seemed out of character for December. Officer Holden, though usually abrupt and rude, had never been a violent man. He, too, had acted out of character.

Eli's pressing business in Georgetown was exceeded by the anxiety of how to report the death of the lighthouse inspector. As he rowed, he tried to balance the prophet Micah's call to do justice with the command to love mercy. Eli decided that Roy Holden did not need to be judged. The kindest thing would be to treat the inspector with mercy, if at all possible.

Along the shore, Eli noticed the old floodgates that used to be opened and closed to allow fresh water into the rice field, and to keep salt water out. In the early 1800s Georgetown was the richest county in the United States. Sixty-two rice plantations bordered Winyah Bay and the four rivers that emptied into the bay. Carolina Gold was the rice grown and exported, making Georgetown the largest supplier of rice in the world.

A series of strong hurricanes at the end of the nineteenth century brought an end to the rice crops. The tide moved as far as fourteen miles from the ocean into the rivers. One particularly powerful storm surge put the city of Georgetown twelve feet under water. A massive storm could flood the entire area with seawater for miles. Salt water killed the rice. The fields were flooded so often that the plantation owners lost their fortunes.

Many sold their land to wealthy northern investors. Some of the Georgetown old-timers referred to it as the second northern invasion.

At Frazier Point, Eli moved the boat across the bay toward the Sampit River. The Great Pee Dee, the Black, and the Waccamaw Rivers entered further to the north.

An hour later, Eli drifted past the old cypress pilings from the original wharf. His trip into Georgetown had been pleasant and relatively quick. As he had hoped, the tidal current and the steady breeze brought him to the harbor in good time. He paused at the old dock for a moment.

Eli loved the sea. It had been a part of his life since his childhood in Odessa. When he had immigrated, it was only natural that he should choose to live close to the ocean. Being a foreigner made the transition to the Lowcountry of South Carolina a challenge and being Jewish could have occasioned even more difficulties. But Eli came to Georgetown because it was home to his uncle, his only remaining relative as far as he knew.

Eli dropped the sail and mast at the mouth of the Sampit River, raised the daggerboard, and repositioned the oars. His back to the bow, he rowed into Georgetown Harbor.

Georgetown had been Eli's home for only 15 years. In some ways it reminded him of his home in the Ukraine. As a boy, Eli had gone to the wharves to watch the tall ships being loaded with grain for voyages across the Black Sea. At the docks in Georgetown, tall-masted schooners, which in bygone years were loaded with indigo and rice, now held cargo of lumber and cotton. Though Georgetown was smaller in size, like Odessa, it was a community tied to the sea.

No less important to Eli, Georgetown, like Odessa, had a significant Jewish community, which included his uncle. Since before the Revolutionary War, numerous Jewish citizens had lived in Georgetown. Beth Elohim, the local synagogue, was established in 1904. Jews had served in positions as mayor and as town council representatives. Several prominent businessmen were heads of Jewish families. Though there was some anti-Semitism, even racists like the Ku Klux Klan and bigots like Pitchfork Ben Tillman had little influence on the Jewish community in Georgetown.

Eli noticed that the lighthouse tender ship *Cypress* was preparing to leave the harbor. The crew was bustling on the deck. He was hesitant as he rowed toward the boat.

The first mate spoke, "Solomon, have you seen Officer Holden this morning?"

"No, not this morning."

"Neither have any of us. He left here yesterday in the dinghy. He was drunk, and he had a new bottle with him. We've already reported him as missing to the Coast Guard in Charleston. They'll contact the Lighthouse Service. They'll be searching for him from Cape Fear to Charleston. I'm afraid he has come to no good. No telling where he is."

"No telling," responded Eli.

"We need to cast off. We're headed back to Charleston for Christmas. See you next trip."

Eli was relieved. Holden's absence had already been reported. He really had not said much at all because he didn't have to.

He moored the skiff to the dock behind Richard Meade's store. He had arrived in Georgetown in time to walk to the Saturday morning *Shabbes* service at Beth Elohim.

As he left the boat, Samuel called out to him in a deep, pleasant voice. "Glad to see oonuh, Mr. Eli. T'ings okay out at de light?"

The two friends looked at each other knowingly.

"Can I hep oonuh wit s'plies?" asked Samuel.

"I have a list," said the Ukrainian, removing a torn piece of paper from his shirt pocket. "I am going for a walk. I'll be back."

"I be getting' oonah's stuff up and put it in de boat. Storm comin', Mr. Eli. Best not tarry."

"Yes. I'll be back soon. I'll leave when the tide turns. Thank you, Samuel."

Eli thought about his friend, Samuel. He was an old man, a former slave, who had seen hard times. He walked with an awkward limp and used a walking stick, but he still had strong arms and shoulders. He had worked for Richard Meade and put up with a lot of abuse. Some people in Georgetown took Samuel for granted, but as far as Eli was concerned, Samuel was a wise man. He was surely right about the storm that was brewing. He also had an instinctive understanding of people that was rare.

Eli slung his cloth bag over his shoulder and made his way to Front Street. The business area of Georgetown was decorated for Christmas. Electric lights gleamed in a few storefronts. Eli wondered if he would ever see electricity on North Island.

Branches of pine, cedar, and magnolia were tied with ribbons to lampposts. The doors of homes along Eli's way to the synagogue displayed evergreen wreaths. Odd, thought Eli, Christians speak of this season as one of waiting for the expected Messiah. Then they make such a fuss over the birth of one baby who became an itinerate teacher. Jews wait for the Messiah year-round.

Eli took the yarmulke and prayer shawl from the cloth bag as he prepared to enter the synagogue.

He saw the elderly Mr. Heiman Kaminski find his place. Mr. Kaminski had come to South Carolina from Prussia when he was only fifteen years old, in the early 1850s. He fought for the Confederate Army during the Civil War. Since then he had become a successful businessman and one of the wealthiest and finest citizens of Georgetown.

Mr. Kaminski had befriended Eli's uncle, giving him his first job in this country. He had also helped Eli secure the job of lighthouse keeper on North Island, even though Eli had only recently become a United States citizen.

Eli was rarely able to attend services at the synagogue but participating in worship was a joyful experience for him. He loved the Hebrew language though he did not speak it well. He usually prayed from memory in Hebrew and read the Torah each day though his understanding of the Hebrew was elementary. In the synagogue, prayers and readings in Hebrew were meaningful as he followed along in the prayer book. Eli sat near the back of the synagogue. He knew few people but felt a kinship with all.

Following the service, he greeted Mr. Kaminski and the rabbi, the only two people he knew by name though he recognized several faces. The president of the synagogue introduced himself.

"Welcome. I am the president here."

"I am Eli Solomon." The lighthouse keeper spoke with an accent.

"You must be new in Georgetown. I don't believe we've met."

"No, but I am not new. I have been here fifteen years."

"Oh, I see. You're just not an observant Jew."

Eli did not respond.

"Well, I hope you'll come back," the president said, moving on to shake another hand.

Eli walked away from Beth Elohim to the nearby Jewish cemetery. The synagogue president's quick judgment troubled him. After all, he had rowed and sailed for four hours this very morning to come to *Shabbes* service. Of course, his hard work was a violation of *Shabbes*. He did the best he could with a faith that was not well suited to the duties of a lighthouse keeper.

Eli visited his uncle's grave. After the fire that took his home and his family, his father's younger brother was his family. Uncle Mordecai had lost his wife and infant child on the long journey to America. When Eli first arrived from Odessa, his uncle had made a home for him. Eli was grateful for this man who had seemed to understand his grief. He had given him a haven when Eli needed it most.

From his pocket, Eli took the stone-like polished piece of green glass he had found on the beach at North Island. Following Jewish custom, he placed it on his uncle's marker, an appropriate gift from the sea for a man who loved the sea. The granite headstone was engraved:

P'n

Mordecai Solomon
Born In Ukraine
Died July 1916

As far as Eli knew, his Uncle Mordecai had been his last remaining relative. His uncle was a man of encouragement. He understood the difficulties of being an immigrant, adjusting to a new culture.

He recalled the words his uncle spoke when Eli had received a promotion to the position of Keeper of the North Island Light Station. Paraphrasing the words of Hebrew scripture, he had asked, "Who knows but that you have come to Georgetown for just such a time as this?"

Those words were first spoken in ancient times by another Uncle Mordecai to his niece, Hadassah, when she became Esther, Queen of Persia. Recorded in the Book of Esther in the Hebrew scriptures, her Uncle Mordecai had said, "Who knows but that you have come to the kingdom for just such a time as this."

Eli breathed a prayer of gratitude for his Uncle Mordecai, who had given a spoken blessing to his nephew, the lighthouse keeper.

Eli walked to Meade's General Store. He would have preferred to make his purchases from Mr. Kaminski. Meade referred to the owner of the larger, more profitable general stores as "that Hebrew." Because the lighthouse service had a contract with Meade, Eli had no choice. He must purchase his supplies from Meade. As he entered the store, Eli tipped his lighthouse service cap.

"Solomon, what can I do for a Jew on the day before Christmas Eve Sunday?"

"I came for supplies. I gave the list to Samuel."

"Hells bells, that boy can't read." It was a strange expression to Eli. Did Hades have bells? And how could Samuel be called boy if he was old enough to be Meade's father?

Samuel came limping awkwardly through the backdoor of the store. "Evuht'ing in de boat, Mr. Eli. All set."

"Nigga', you know you can't read." Meade blurted. "Give me that list." With that Meade snatched the list from Samuel's hand and went to the dock to check the order.

"Mr. Meade feelin' poorly. His baby girl is on de steamer coming from up north. De steamer was due yestidy. She's running a day late. Mr. Meade worried sick."

Eli thought about Samuel's understanding of Richard Meade though Meade seemed to have no interest in understanding Samuel.

"Well, bless Pat, the dumb nigga' got it right. He asked somebody to read it to him. He can't read a lick."

As if to justify himself, Meade pushed the newspaper *The Georgetown Times* across the store counter toward Samuel. "Read this," he demanded.

Samuel paused, looking at Meade, "Mr. Meade, I can't."

"No, and you can't read the Jew's supply list either."

"Yes, suh, I can. I can't read readin'. I jest can read writin'."

"Dumb nigga'." He dismissed Samuel and turned to Eli, "What else, Solomon?"

"That's all. What can I do for you, Mr. Meade?"

"Sign the ticket. It's the only way the federal government will pay me."

Eli signed, in neat cursive handwriting. "Can I do anything else for you?"

Meade's face turned red, and his eyes welled with tears. "Keep that light burning, Solomon. My daughter is on the Clyde Line steamer *Cherokee* from New York. Of course, you wouldn't understand. You've never had a daughter to worry about."

Eli didn't say anything.

Meade continued his rant, "I bought the ticket from Kaminski. It was hard enough to give him my money. I sure don't want to lose my daughter because of him. The steamer was supposed to be here yesterday. My wife is worried to death. But you wouldn't understand. You don't have a wife or a child. Just keep that light burning so they can make it through the channel. "

Eli reached out his right hand to shake Richard Meade's hand. Meade turned away with one last snarl, "Do your damn job, Solomon. Get my daughter home."

Eli walked to the door at the back of the store. Samuel met him at the dock.

"Oonuh ain't had not'ing to eat, Mr. Eli. I fix a bag."

"Thank you," Eli accepted the brown paper bag. The two men shook hands, and Eli boarded the skiff for the thirteen-mile trip back to North Island.

As he used an oar to push away from the dock, Samuel called out, "Best hurry, Mr. Eli, Storm's comin'. Comin' soon."

The oars dug deep in the gray waters of Winyah Bay as Eli made his way toward Frazier Point. Facing the stern, his arms pulled hard to reach the current moving with the receding tide out toward the Atlantic. A half-hour later, the wind blew directly in his face. He turned around in the skiff, lowered the daggerboard, set the mast, and unfurled the sail. The sheet caught the wind as Eli fixed an oar, now the rudder, in the rear oarlock. The skiff picked up speed, and Eli had time to eat the apple, cheese, sardines, and bread Samuel had given him. He also had time to reflect.

Meade was just Meade. Whatever the pain in his life, it had made him a bitter man. Eli had encountered people like Richard Meade and Roy Holden all through his life. In Odessa, there had also been Jew-haters. Some of them may have been responsible for burning his home and taking his family from him. Eli would never know what caused the fire.

Meade was desperate. Eli could not save his daughter. Only God could do that. But Eli would keep the light burning to guide the captain of the *Cherokee* into Winyah Bay.

Samuel was the only person in Georgetown he could depend on. He had cordial relationships with some members of the Jewish community. He just wasn't with them enough to feel close. Samuel, though, was always there and always a friend. He had never seen Samuel anywhere but on dry ground except when he came out to the inlet to fish. Just from that, Eli could tell that Samuel understood the sea. Samuel was a wise man. Eli regarded him almost as a brother.

You're not an observant Jew. The stinging words of the synagogue president returned to his mind.

Though Eli had tried to make peace with his life as keeper of the light, the confrontation by the president of the synagogue wounded his spirit with the truth. He could not attend *Shabbes* services each week, and he certainly failed in other responsibilities of the faith.

I'm not an observant Jew? What does it mean to be observant? Eli wondered.

A family of dolphins swam alongside the skiff as it glided across the open water. On the opposite shore, he could see a large buck and two does skipping along the beach. They were wet, and Eli knew they had crossed the water from Rabbit Island to Old Hobcaw Barony. If Eli was anything, he was an observant Jew. Maybe he could not observe all of the traditions, but he paid attention to the world around him. What he observed now told him that the storm was near.

Beyond Mohawk Island, a wild boar swam for higher ground. Now in the dark sky, a bald eagle and a pair of osprey soared inland. The storm was going to be unusual for December. Eli prayed for the steamer, for Richard Meade's daughter, and for strength as the wind turned, becoming a strong headwind.

Dropping the mast, Eli stowed the sail, shifted his position, and fixed the oars. In the distance, he heard the rumbling of thunder. Moving as close to the islands as he could, he rowed the skiff toward the lighthouse. Facing the stern of the small boat, he pulled against the oars with all of his might. Darkness will come early tonight, he thought. I must light the lamp as soon as I reach the beach.

For two hours more, Eli struggled against the wind. The tide was of little help as the small boat broke through the waves building in the bay. The dark water was covered with whitecaps.

This is like rowing in the open ocean, Eli thought. He kept the oar handles wet, but still, his hands blistered.

Out of the corner of his eye, he caught a glimpse of the little blond-headed girl running along the shore. When he turned to look, he saw the old African, black as night with white hair and beard, waving as if encouraging him to row harder.

Thunder echoed across the water. Lightning flashed in the distance. Trees along the shore bent and swayed in the gale. And then, within a hundred yards of the lighthouse, Eli simultaneously heard a deafening clap of thunder and saw a blinding flash of lightning.

The boat shuddered as the sound reverberated across the water. Eli pivoted in the skiff to see the top of the tall loblolly pine, the one he had wanted to cut, ignite like a giant match. The dry tree was at once consumed in flames. It split in half. Eli watched in horror as half of the blazing tree fell across the roof of the fuel shed.

Another bolt of lightning ripped through the black sky as Eli beached the boat. Melchizedek met him on the beach, barking but ready to help. Gathering the wooden box of the most perishable supplies while trying to collect his thoughts, he scrambled to the keeper's house. The dog had already herded the Nubians to the highest available spot, up on the porch. The guineas were nowhere to be seen.

As he reached the steps, Eli heard the first of the kerosene cans explode. And then another and another. The explosions from the fuel shed sounded like an artillery battle in the Crimean war. The goats huddled together against the outside wall of the house. From the covered porch, Eli watched helplessly as the entire supply of fuel fed the inferno. And then the rain came – hard.

Eli ran through the sand back to the boat, the rain stinging his face. The old African with white hair materialized again and handed him the second box of supplies. The man attempted to say something in a loud voice using gutturals that Eli could not understand. Then the strange man, who had again been a godsend, disappeared over the dunes into the forest.

Holding the box under one arm, Eli grabbed the mooring rope fastened to the bow of the skiff. Pulling with all of his might, he dragged the boat out of the water up onto the dunes.

Now the fuel shed was reduced to a brick pit of burning embers. The blazing pine tree had set the dry brush of the nearby woods on fire. Though it was still burning, the heavy, blowing rain would soon put it out.

Eli had a more pressing problem. *How to light the lamp in the lighthouse?*

He tried again to gather his thoughts as he rubbed his blistered hands. The entire supply of kerosene had been destroyed.

The steamer *Cherokee* with Meade's daughter on board was somewhere out in the Atlantic. The storm was a strong December nor'easter with gale-force winds. He had to find a way to make the light work. There would certainly be no oil in the double-wicked lamp because he had left it to burn itself out when he went to Georgetown before dawn.

But then, he remembered, *There is another lamp.*

He hurried inside the house, gathering food and matches into the cloth bag. He pulled on the rain slicker. He saw the menorah in the window, and quickly lit five candles, mumbling the prayer as he did. Then, he picked up the single wick kerosene lamp next to the Torah and *The Pink Book* from the nightstand. He shook the lamp. There was some kerosene, not enough, but some.

Back on the porch, he whistled loudly. Slogging through water already ankle-deep, he went to the lighthouse and waited as Melchizedek herded the Nubians inside the tower. In the darkness, he climbed the

124 stairs to the top. The wind drove the rain like bullets against the lantern room windows.

Eli felt his way to the double-wicked lamp. It was, as expected, completely out of fuel. He considered placing the table lamp inside the Fresnel lens, but the single wick would not give enough light. Carefully, he poured the precious liquid from the table lamp into the other. The double-wicked lamp in place, he struck an official lighthouse service match, lit the wicks, and lowered the torpedo weight. The lens began to turn, casting a beam into the gloom.

Eli took the yarmulke from the cloth bag. From the window of the lantern room, he could see the menorah shining brightly in the window of the keeper's house. Then for the second time, on the fifth night of Hanukkah, Eli prayed, this time more slowly.

> Blessed are You, Lord our God, King of the Universe,
> Who has sanctified us with His commandments,
> And commanded us to kindle the light of Hanukkah.
> Blessed are You, Lord our God, King of the Universe,
> Who performed miracles for our fathers in those days,
> and at this time.

Then, Eli added the words of Psalm 21:

> The Lord is my light and my salvation—whom shall I fear?

Soaked and exhausted, Eli thought, *There might be enough oil for an hour. The light will not burn through the night. Maybe it will burn long enough to bring the Cherokee and Meade's daughter safely home.*

Eli took one more look at the menorah in the window below. The five candles were burning low and would soon be out. He sat against the wall of the lantern room atop the Georgetown light and watched the light circling above his head.

There is not nearly enough oil, he thought.

And then with the wind and the rain pounding as loudly as the throbbing pain in his weary head, Eli Solomon slept.

Chapter Seventeen

Professor Rosen:

The plantation owners of All Saints Parish were intent on educating their slaves in the Christian faith. Regular worship services were held on each plantation twice each month by a traveling Episcopal priest. The slaves brought with them to America a rich background of African religious expression. They did not so much convert to Christianity as they adapted Christianity to their previous beliefs.

The planters encouraged obedience of slaves to their masters, coupled with the hope that those who suffered on earth would be rewarded in heaven. The slaves, however, were as concerned about freedom in this world as with salvation in the next. This desire for freedom was evident in their prayer meetings accompanied by singing, shouting, and ecstatic experience. Worship was not passive listening. Worship was active participation. Sermons and prayers elicited a verbal response from the congregation.

They wanted to hear about deliverance from oppression: Daniel in the lions' den, the Hebrew children in the fiery furnace, David killing Goliath, and Moses leading the people out of slavery with plagues visited on the slaveholders.

Samuel Pringle was a freed slave. Deep in his soul, he exercised that freedom within the narrow constraints of the society in which he now lived. Like many other Gullah people, Samuel's freedom was liberty of mind, heart, and soul.

Saturday, December 23, 1916, continued

At dusk on Saturday evening, Samuel Pringle leaned against the post on the porch in front of his shanty. He packed tobacco into his corncob pipe, shielded a kitchen match from the freshening breeze, and lit the brown leaves, puffing until flames leapt from the charred bowl.

He smoked and watched as a violent storm pushed across Winyah Bay and over Georgetown. Thunder rumbled, echoing across the water. Lightning bolts ignited the sky. Palmetto palms shook their mop heads of dry rustling fronds. Great live oak trees gracefully swayed, their arms fringed with Spanish moss. Tall loblolly pines bent dancing before the strong wind.

Winyah Bay showed whitecaps as far as the eye could see. Just beyond the wind-whipped marsh grass, the Sampit River was at flood tide. Pelting rain pitted the dark surface of the water, and then sheets of blowing rain obscured the river altogether. This was the dramatic change that Samuel had expected.

Mr. Eli heard de prophet wave; know'd 'twas bound to come.

Most folks in Georgetown would have considered the storm that lashed the Lowcountry on Saturday night a negative occurrence. Some would think only of the property damage. How much would repairs cost? Some would think of the fear that such a weather event would bring to old people and to children. As a matter of fact, Samuel could see Maggie through her window trying to calm Sally. Others, like the preacher at the Mizpah African Methodist Episcopal Church, would speak of the storm as the wrath of God.

Samuel Pringle regarded the storm as a good thing. It was as if the whole county had been suffering from a high fever. The cooling rain had broken the fever. The rhythm of nature had been restored. Water supplies like Eli Solomon's cistern were refreshed. December could be December, like it was supposed to be.

Samuel climbed the steps to his shanty. He took off his clothes and crawled into bed. He prayed that the steamer *Cherokee* would bring Mr. Meade's daughter home safely for Christmas. He prayed for Maggie and for Eli, and then he drifted off to sleep listening to the rain on his tin roof as the storm subsided.

Chapter Eighteen

Sunday, December 24, 1916, Georgetown

Samuel was up early, long before dawn. The Sunday before Christmas was a day when most folks, Black and white, would be in church. They would hear the story about Mary and Joseph traveling all the way to Bethlehem; Mary, great with child, riding on a donkey; shepherds scared to death when all heaven broke loose; angels singing in the sky; and wise men bringing presents to baby Jesus who was wrapped in swaddling clothes, lying in a manger.

Nobody believed in Jesus more than Samuel did, but he rarely went to church, except maybe for a funeral or a wedding. After Rachel died, just going into the church building made him remember her and all that sorrow. He preferred to spend his Sunday mornings doing things to help somebody else. There were plenty of folks who needed help, but Samuel had two people on his mind this Sunday morning.

Across the sandy track on the Gullah Line, he could see Maggie Howard through her kitchen window, up and stirring around. She was always in his mind since she had sat close to him holding his arm on the porch. He admired her, not only because of her beauty but also because of her spunk. Maggie was a wise woman, completely dedicated to caring for her woman-child, Sally. He looked forward to having supper at her house on Christmas night.

Samuel had also been thinking about Eli Solomon as he watched and listened to the storm roll in. When he was in town on Saturday, Eli didn't say anything about Officer Roy Holden. Samuel knew that something had happened, maybe even something bad. He checked the sky to the east after the storm had passed and was relieved to see the North Island light circling as always. But for some reason unclear to Samuel, he felt like this was a day he should row to the inlet to check on the keeper of the North Island Lighthouse.

The December air was much cooler on Sunday morning. When Samuel left his shanty, he wore his coat, a wool jacket that had belonged to John Howard. Maggie had given it to him after John died. Wearing it reminded him of John and made him think of Maggie.

Under a clear dark sky, he rowed away from the cypress dock. The stars were still bright, the moon barely visible. Except for the sound of his oars dipping in the water, the Sampit was silent. Not even the lumber mill operated on Sunday morning. Occasionally ceasing his rowing, Samuel drifted along, enjoying the early morning quiet.

As he approached the dock behind Meade's General Store, he was surprised to see an eerie light coming from under the backdoor.

Whut might dat be? he thought.

He tied up his boat, knotting the rope to a cleat. He lifted himself from the boat onto the dock, and using his cedar walking stick, stood to his feet. He moved cautiously to the door. He turned the handle, and the door opened.

"Mr. Meade, oonuh in here?" he called.

He heard steps, and Richard Meade appeared holding a lantern. "Nigga', you scared me. What are you doing sneaking around here on Sunday morning?"

"I jest be passin' by 'n seen de light on. Thought somethin' might be wrong."

"Passing by going where?"

"Goin' out to check on Mr. Eli see if he alright after dat storm."

"If that ain't the stupidest thing I ever heard of."

"Oonuh alright, Mr. Meade?"

'Yes, my daughter got home early this morning. The *Cherokee* came in safely. I tried to go back to sleep, but I couldn't. My wife said we need a few more things for Christmas, so I came on in to get them. Mostly groceries, sweet potatoes, and flour."

"Yes, suh, I be goin' den."

"Nigga', ain't you afraid to be out there in the bay in the dark?"

"No, suh, I ain't 'fraid. Be fust light 'fo long. 'Sides I know dat watta'."

"Well, if you're going all the way out to the lighthouse, tell Solomon I want to see him next time he's in town."

"Yes, suh, sho will."

"You ought'a be more careful sneaking around like that. You might get shot."

"Yes, suh."

Samuel left through the backdoor. Back in his blue boat, he rowed out into Winyah Bay. He caught the swift current of the outgoing tide as it flowed from the four rivers swollen overnight by the storm.

As he passed Rabbit Island, the first signs of dawn appeared on Winyah Bay. He pulled in the oars and swung his body around toward

221

the bow of the boat drifting with the current. He used a single oar as a rudder to hold his course, letting the tide carry him to the east.

To the right, Samuel saw a doe grazing on a slight knoll above the water. He saw something that reminded him of the time when he was a slave. It was one of the old gates used to control the flow of fresh water to nourish the rice. He remembered the hurricanes that flooded the fields with seawater time and again until all of the Carolina Gold rice was destroyed, and the plantations were put out of business.

To the east, gray clouds hung over the ocean and reflected the beam of the Georgetown light. The thick clouds, the last vestiges of the storm the night before, made for a glorious sunrise. The vast sky became a work of art, first a deep purple that gradually lightened. Gray clouds turned deep pink and grew brighter, signaling the upward approach of the sun. There was a burst of red just before the large orange sun rose above the horizon.

Just ahead off the bow to his right, he saw something floating in the water. He steered the blue boat close enough to reach out and grab a stray oar. He recognized it immediately as one that belonged to the skiff used by Eli Solomon. He wondered what had happened to bring it so far away from the lighthouse. He knew the light had burned through the night and had guided the *Cherokee* safely into harbor. But how did Eli Solomon lose an oar?

Samuel turned back around in the boat facing the stern, locked his oars, and began rowing more purposefully. The stray oar from Eli's skiff made his mission more urgent. He wanted to know that his friend was alright.

Close to Shell Island, an osprey soared overhead, plunged into the bay, and seized a large fish in her sharp talons. The fish was a good-sized spot tail bass. As the osprey retreated to a nearby tree to enjoy breakfast, another large bird attacked the osprey to steal the fish. It was a larger bald eagle. In the skirmish overhead, the spot tail was inadvertently released, dropping straight into the stern of Samuel's blue boat. "I reckon hit jest ain't your day, Buh fish," said Samuel, laughing out loud.

As Samuel neared the ocean, a pod of dolphins followed in his wake, arching on one side of the blue boat and then the other as if they were children playing tag. When the lighthouse was in view, Samuel saw Eli standing on the beach with the dog. The lighthouse keeper was waving excitedly.

Chapter Nineteen

Professor Rosen:

In Hebrew, *chai* is the word for life. A classic Jewish concept explains that human life is sacred. The account of the creation of Adam and Eve, in the divine image (Genesis 1:26-27), introduces the idea that human life is special.

All of nature is special - light, sea, land, sun, moon, and stars; all plants, fish, birds, animals, insects — all is the incredible handiwork of the Creator. Yet there is something different about a human being.

One difference we see in the account in Genesis is that while all other living creatures were created in large numbers, the first human being, Adam, was alone. The Talmud states that the fact that Adam was alone is to teach us the significance of each individual.

A classic Jewish concept explains that the will to do evil is competing with the intention to do good. The great Jewish teacher Maimonides put forth the idea that the entire world is equally balanced between good and evil. Each of us as an individual, is equally balanced between good and evil. If we make one good action, we tip the balance for ourselves and for the entire world to the side of good. As the rabbis taught, a single act of goodness and kindness will bring redemption.

The sanctity of life is one of the most important concepts in the Jewish worldview. This idea is expressed, clearly and simply, in the sixth of the Ten Commandments: Thou shall not murder (Exodus 20:13).

Just as all people and all nations have had times of disregard for others, so Jews, too, have made plenty of mistakes individually and nationally. However, the Jewish people have always stood for the value of human life. Despite horrendous persecutions down through the ages, the Jewish people have maintained a level of compassion that exceeded the surrounding civilizations.

One of the most significant expressions of the value of life is found in the Talmud.

> *He who saves one life... is as if he saves an entire world.*
> *He who destroys a life... is as if he destroys an entire world.*

Even with the persecution and grief within his own experience, the sanctity of life and the redemptive power of goodness were deeply held beliefs for Eli Solomon.

Sunday, December 24, 1916, North Island

Rays of the sun piercing the clouds over the Atlantic awakened Eli. As he came to consciousness from a deep sleep, he was astounded to see the lighthouse still sending a strong beam across the waves. He struggled to his feet, his back and shoulders aching, his hands blistered. The storm had moved inland overnight. The sky was brightening to the south. He peered across the gray-green ocean toward the horizon.

No sign of the steamer, he thought, *but the light is still burning. How? There was so little oil in the lamp last night when he first lit the wicks, not nearly enough to last through the night.*

Eli extinguished the double wick. He noticed a dead seagull on the rim of the lighthouse. The bird had been blown into the tower during the gale. Eli stepped out onto the circular metal walkway high above the ground and removed the limp, feathered body.

Another loss of life, he thought. *And now I am ritually unclean because I handled a dead bird. Another wasted life, and another violation of the Torah.*

Looking back toward Winyah Bay, he saw broken trees strewn along both banks. His eyes followed the shoreline to the place he had beached the skiff. His boat was gone! The storm surge had taken it away.

Turning back toward the ocean, he saw the beach littered with debris. Gulls were picking through the remains, searching for their breakfast. Beyond the jetties, brown pelicans were gliding close to the calming water, looking for mullet. The storm had passed. The light had burned brightly all through the night.

But now, there was no kerosene. There was no skiff. There was no sign of any other boat. The keeper of the lighthouse was in a predicament.

Unclean as he was, he paused to put on his yarmulke and tallith, and to offer his morning prayer.

Then Eli moved down the stone steps as Melchizedek urged the goats from their temporary overnight quarters back to ground level. The guineas fluttered down from the live oak. In the cool morning air, Eli inspected the grounds. The fire had destroyed the fuel shed. The skiff was gone. The cistern was replenished. The house was unharmed. Eli washed his hands and changed into dry clothes. He rubbed salve on his sore hands. He ate cheese and bread and pondered his dilemma. He would simply do what he could do. He read from Exodus 31:7.

> *Be strong and courageous.*
> *Do not be afraid or terrified.*
> *For the Lord your God goes with you;*
> *He will never leave you nor forsake you.*

The truth of that scripture had been displayed. A little oil had burned much longer than expected. What had happened on North Island overnight was the miracle of Hanukkah repeated. There was no other way to understand it.

Eli gathered his cleaning supplies. Even if he had no kerosene, he would clean the light as usual. Climbing back to the top of the tower, he completed his work. The sun now glistened on the ocean, as if the sea had been scrubbed clean as well.

Turning back toward Winyah Bay, Eli could hardly believe his eyes. A rowboat was approaching the island. He hurried down the steps and ran to the beach, hoping to summon whoever was in the boat. But the bright blue boat was already near the shore.

Samuel raised a large hand in greeting and shouted, "Mr. Eli, I come to see 'bout oonuh."

"Glad to see you." It was the second miracle of the day.

"Found dis oar," said Samuel. "oonuh lose it?"

"My boat was lost in the storm surge. No sign of it anywhere."

"Maybe we fin' it somewhere up yonder."

Eli showed Samuel the burned fuel shed. "I've got to have more fuel."

"Mr. Meade got plenty. We git some from de sto'."

"I need a few things from the house."

Eli got his Lighthouse Service jacket, a half loaf of bread, and some goat cheese. He put more salve on his palms and wrapped his blistered hands in clean cotton rags. He grabbed a double ration of corn to scatter for the guineas. From the half ration of salt pork left by Roy

Holden, he took a ham, a slab of bacon, and another scrap of the non-kosher meat.

Back on the beach, Eli handed the food to Samuel already in the boat. "The ham and the bacon are for you," he said.

Sure enough, Samuel had rescued one oar found floating in the bay. But not the skiff. They shoved off for the thirteen-mile trip back to Georgetown.

Eli flipped a scrap of pork to his dog. Melchizedek stood on the beach, savoring the treat as the two men rowed away from the island.

"Guard the goats," Eli shouted at the dog in Yiddish.

The boat was equipped with double oarlocks and three oars. With an extra oar from the skiff there were two pair, unmatched, but not unlike the two oarsmen. Black man and white man, Ukrainian and African, Jew and Gentile, each named for a Hebrew prophet – Eli and Samuel rowed together as one.

As Eli had suspected, his companion was no stranger to the water. He walked with an awkward limp, but his boatmanship was flawless. His powerful arms and shoulders matched the strength of Eli. Having already rowed from Georgetown out to the lighthouse since early morning, Samuel showed no signs of fatigue.

Samuel noticed several redwing blackbirds perched on tall reeds in the salt marsh. He remembered the birds in the rice fields in the days of his youth. His mother told him that the blackbirds with the red blaze on their wings were a reminder that fire was a gift from the Lord. He thought it best not to mention that to Eli so soon after the fuel shed had been destroyed by fire.

Further up the bay, the salt marsh receded, giving way to another stretch of sand dunes. Eli and Samuel saw the Black man with white hair and beard standing on the dunes. A small man, he beckoned to them, hand held high. Samuel turned the boat to the beach.

The two Black men embraced. Samuel shouted in Gullah beyond the understanding of Eli. After a few minutes of cacophony, Samuel returned to the boat and took the slab of bacon and the spot tail fish to the other man.

"Merry Christmas," he shouted loudly.

The two Black men gestured their goodbyes.

As Eli and Samuel continued their journey, Samuel explained that the strange man was his cousin, Rupert, the last of his family. He explained that when he was a boy, Rupert had the fever that left him deaf and mute.

"He can't hear hit thunder," he said.

They had thought each had died in a hurricane years before. Rupert had lived in a hut in the forest of North Island before the massive storm. He had tied himself in the branch of a live oak tree to weather the storm. After the storm, he was the only person left alive on the island except for the keeper of the lighthouse.

Rupert told Samuel that now he kept an eye on the current lighthouse keeper. He assured him that Eli was a good man.

Eli and Samuel rowed on toward Georgetown.

Eli asked about Rupert. "I see your cousin is not such a tall man."

"No, suh. Dat feber lef' him def 'n dum. Hit lef' him stunted too."

"But his feet; they are so large."

"Yes, suh, Rupert ain't neber had no shoes. His feets just flatten' out and git big. Rupert gots big feets and a big heart."

Eli said no more about his mysterious North Island neighbor.

At Malady Bush Island, they found Eli's boat, no worse for the wear. The other oar was secured inside. They tied the mooring rope and towed the smaller boat behind them, rowing together across Winyah Bay. Along the way, they took turns eating the bread and cheese that Eli had brought.

As they rowed, Eli explained what happened during the storm, how the fuel shed had been destroyed, how the light had burned miraculously through the night.

Samuel told about how he had grown up on the water. During slavery, he had been a taster and tender on the plantation. His job was to taste the water and tend the floodgates. If the water was salty, as it is at high tide, he closed the floodgates. If the water was fresh flowing down from the rivers, he opened the gates to flood the rice fields.

Samuel told about how he worked for the Atlantic Coast Lumber Company until a band saw got in a bind and bucked, throwing a half-sawed log into his groin, crushing his thigh. When it finally healed, he could hardly walk. The company wouldn't take him back, so he got a job working for Richard Meade.

Rarely did Eli ask questions of other people. But he asked Samuel, "How old are you?"

Samuel laughed, "Lawd, don't know. 'Bout old as dirt is, and Rupert two years older 'dan dat."

The Black man paused his rowing long enough to light his pipe. After a few puffs Samuel asked Eli about Roy Holden.

Eli waited. Samuel was the only person he knew to whom he could tell the story. He trusted Samuel with the truth. He told Samuel about the corset and what he suspected.

Samuel took a long draw on his pipe before he spoke. "Fear is terrible t'ing. Evhbody jest want to be loved. Gawd loves evhbody, even them dat don't know hit."

"He tried to kill me," said Eli. "He thought I had information that would destroy his career and his reputation."

Eli went on to explain exactly what happened, how Roy Holden had been in a drunken rage, how Holden came after Eli with a shotgun, how Melchizedek had protected him, how Roy Holden was knocked into the pond by the dog, and how the three alligators ripped apart the Lighthouse Service officer.

"Your Cousin Rupert was there. He is a witness. He saw the whole thing."

In the harbor, Eli saw the steamer *Cherokee* safely anchored. It had made it through the jetties sometime during the stormy night. There was no sign of the Lighthouse Service tender boat.

At the dock behind Meade's General Store, the two men moored both the rowboat and the skiff. They went into the storeroom to get four cases of kerosene from the back room. Hanging on a peg, they saw a white sheet and hood. The two men, Jew and African-American, exchanged knowing looks without a word.

They secured the cases of kerosene in the skiff. Eli wrote out a bill and signed it.

Samuel said, "Mr. Meade want oonuh t' come to his place."

Eli was reluctant. He had rather wait at the dock for the tide to turn before taking the skiff back to the island. Now that he had seen the white sheet and hood, he didn't want to ever see Meade again

"Come on along, Mr. Eli. It be fine."

Richard Meade's home was a short walk from his store, but for Samuel, any walk was long. Slowly the prophets, Eli and Samuel, walked together. A bright cardinal chirped from the bough of a magnolia tree. "Redbird singin' a happy song," remarked Samuel. "Somet'ing happy gonna' be done happen." The Meade home was decorated for Christmas. A large wreath of pine and magnolia leaves accented with apples and lemons graced the door.

A servant opened the door to the two men. "Y'all wait right here on dis porch," she instructed. In the foyer, Eli saw a large red cedar tree decorated with ornaments. Beneath the tree were presents wrapped in colorful paper. He had seen Christmas trees before when he lived with his uncle. The tree still struck him as odd. Why not just let it live where it grew? Why bring a cedar tree inside a house to die? Christians were a difficult lot to understand.

Meade appeared at the door. He was smiling. It was the third miracle of the day.

"Well, Solomon, you did it. You kept the light burning and brought my daughter home."

Eli did not respond. He knew he had done nothing except to light a small amount of oil. The rest had been divine intervention.

"The captain of the *Cherokee* said he would have never found the channel if it had not been for the lighthouse. He said it was quite a storm. In fact, he said the light saved the ship and all those on board. The captain said that following the light was like the wise men following the star to Bethlehem. Solomon, your light was the light of Christmas."

"I have kerosene from your store, Meade. Samuel helped me load it."

"That's about all he's good for, toting and fetching."

Eli said only, "I wrote out a bill and left it on the counter."

"Solomon, I want you to meet my daughter." A young woman with blond hair and green eyes stepped onto the porch.

"Honey, this man is the lighthouse keeper out on North Island. Solomon, this is my daughter."

Eli tipped his lighthouse service cap but said nothing. Samuel looked down at his own feet.

"Thank you, Mr. Solomon. The light saved all of our lives."

"Honey, you don't have to thank him. It's his job. And don't call him mister, either."

"I am pleased to meet you, Miss Meade," Eli finally said.

"Solomon, we have somebody else who wants to meet you, someone my daughter met on the ship from New York."

Through the door of Richard Meade's house stepped a petite young woman with dark hair and dark eyes. Eli looked at her. Why would she want to see him? For a moment, he just stared. She was vaguely familiar. Did he know her? Then, it was as if he saw a ghost. She looked so much like his wife, so beautiful. He started to reach for her hand but pulled back.

The young woman was even more uncertain. She stared at Eli, unsure of who he was. She took a small step forward.

"This is Eli Solomon, the lighthouse keeper," Meade said.

The young woman took another step forward, reaching out for Eli's trembling hand.

Eli was stunned and speechless. Like fog lifting, he began to realize who this was. Could it be her? Was it too much to hope? As the beautiful young woman held his hand, he could not say anything. Tears flooded his eyes and ran down his cheeks into his beard. He wiped his face with his sleeve. His lips moved, but he could not speak.

"What's the matter with you, Solomon? Cat got your tongue? This girl can't talk much English, but my daughter made out enough to understand that she was looking for you. Do you know her?"

The young woman was curious, gazing at the weathered countenance of the lighthouse keeper. She took another step toward him.

Eli choked back his tears. She looked just like his wife had looked when he got married. She looked just like her mother. Her hair, her form, her eyes, she was the image of her mother. Finally, through quivering lips, he said, "Lenora?"

After a brief moment of hesitation, the young woman exclaimed, "Papa." falling into his arms. Eli caressed her gently, with blistered and bleeding hands, as if she were a fragile China doll.

Father and daughter held each other in a long embrace. Eli wondered, Is this a dream? Is my daughter really here in my arms? It had been so long. They had both come so far to now be reunited on the other side of the world. How is this even possible?

Together they wept. They had never known each other, and they had always known each other. When they finally spoke, it was in Yiddish.

"Solomon, what's all that jabbering about? Is this your daughter? My God. A Jew slept in my house. Solomon, you've been holding out on us."

"She is my child, I thought she was dead, but she is alive." Eli wept out loud. It was the fourth miracle of the day.

After a few moments, Richard Meade's daughter and Samuel began to weep as well. Finally, Meade spoke. "Okay, Solomon, you can go now. I just wanted to tell you that the lighthouse was a Christmas light. It brought my daughter home. You go now. Merry Christmas."

Eli said nothing.

Samuel wiped tears from his eyes. Then, he spoke. "Mr. Meade, de light dat brung yo' daughter home, brung Mr. Eli's daughter home, too. De light dat save one, saved de other'n, too. 'Tis jest one light. De same light shine for evuhbody."

Richard Meade took his daughter's arm. "Let's go inside, Honey, so these people will leave." Meade stepped inside the house behind his daughter. Without looking back, he abruptly closed the door.

Eli and his daughter walked slowly with Samuel hobbling alongside on his walking stick back to the dock behind Richard Meade's store. Eli carried his daughter's luggage, a single tattered bag with tags from several countries attached. The conversation between them was sparse. Words that were spoken were carefully measured and in Yiddish. Both Eli and his daughter, Lenora, realized that they had much to learn about each other. There would be many adjustments for both of them, but the sheer joy of being together overshadowed all of those matters for now.

At the dock behind Meade's store, Lenora noticed the deep blisters on her father's hands. She expressed her concern and asked for ointment and bandages. Eli interpreted for Samuel, who gathered the necessary first aid supplies. With tender young hands, the daughter cleaned and bandaged the rugged hands of her father.

Samuel, who had not understood any of the conversation in the language strange to his ears, spoke in a dialect strange to Lenora's ears.

"Mr. Eli, Take my boat ober to de light. I'll jest use yo' boat 'til oonuh come in again. My boat bigger."

Eli agreed. He and Samuel loaded Lenora's bag into the blue boat. Together they shifted the supplies from the skiff to the blue boat. They said their goodbyes at the dock, and Eli rowed the blue lifeboat into the outgoing current of Winyah Bay.

The thirteen-mile trip seemed to take much less time with Lenora along. She marveled at the beauty of Winyah Bay. She was fascinated by flora and fauna along the shore. As Eli rowed, Lenora laughed and sang.

"At last, I have my child!" Eli thought.

They were greeted by Melchizedek and Rupert when they arrived at the lighthouse. The dog and Lenora hit it off immediately. Rupert helped Eli unload the supplies and the luggage from the blue boat. Eli gave Rupert as much salt pork as he could carry, and the dark man with the white hair disappeared up the path into the forest.

That evening Lenora climbed the lighthouse steps with her father and watched as he filled the lamp. She stood beside him as he said his evening prayers, noticing that he offered them first in halting Hebrew and then in Yiddish. Eli gave thanks for Lenora and her safe passage to Georgetown. She watched as he struck an official Lighthouse Service match and lit the lamp. When she saw the strong beam of light circle across the ocean, she squealed in delight.

Life for Eli was going to be different, and for Lenora, too. They had much to talk about, much to share, much to celebrate, and much to learn.

That night after a light supper of cheese and bread, they lit the sixth candle in the driftwood menorah. Eli recounted the four miracles of the day: the beacon in the lighthouse burning through the night, Samuel coming to rescue him, a smile from Richard Meade, and, best of all, Lenora's arrival. To see his daughter, to have her with him, was a miracle beyond all miracles. Now that he thought about it, there were other miracles, too: the *Cherokee* making it safely into harbor and the discovery that Rupert was not a ghost after all.

Eli was thankful for the many blessings of Hanukkah.

Eli prepared a cot for Lenora in the corner of the house opposite the hammock. They were both tired and slept easily. The dog slept beside Lenora's bed.

Chapter Twenty

Professor Rosen:

For the Christian slaves of All Saints Parish, Christmas was an important day marking the birth of Jesus, the savior who had come to take up the plight of the downtrodden.

On my cab ride to the Cincinnati airport yesterday, I heard on the radio Mahalia Jackson's plaintive and prayerful interpretation of "Sweet Little Jesus Boy" by Robert MacGimsey. The song was published in 1934, but because I was coming to South Carolina, I thought of Samuel Pringle.

The song was composed during hard times and intentionally written in the style of African-American spirituals. His spiritual draws upon a long-standing African-American Protestant theological tradition that began in the time of slavery, merging the Christian Gospel with Black experience. In the spiritual, the story of Jesus' birth was not something in the past, but a present reality.

> Sweet little Jesus boy,
> They made you be born in a manger.
> Sweet little holy child,
> We didn't know who you were.
> Didn't know you'd come to save us, Lord,
> To take our sins away.
> Our eyes were blind. We could not see,
> We didn't know who you were.

Long time ago
You were born,
Born in a manger, Lord,
Sweet little Jesus boy.
The world treats you mean, Lord.
Treats me mean too,
But that's how things are down here.
We didn't know who you were.

The refrain is a reminder that the narrative of the Jesus boy is a universal story. In our world, many children are born out back and grow up hard. God's children have often been treated badly. That has been true in all times and places. MacGimsey ends his song with a call for forgiveness.

You have told us how,
We are trying.
Master, you have shown us how,
Even when you were dying.
Just seems like we can't do right.
Look how we treated you.
But please, Sir, forgive us, Lord.
We didn't know it was you.
Sweet little Jesus boy,
Born a long time ago.
Sweet little holy child,
We didn't know who you were.

For Samuel Pringle, and others like him, the Christian message was that a child born out back in hard times could offer the hope of liberation from fear and the spiritual strength to resist oppression.

Monday, December 25, 1916, Christmas Day, Georgetown

Samuel Pringle was up before dawn. He limped down the sandy path to his cypress dock using the walking stick made from last year's Christmas tree. He paused on the edge of the marsh grass. He looked toward Maggie's house. No lights were on, but as soon as he knew she was up, he was going to see her.

At the dock, he examined the skiff used by Eli Solomon. He admired the modifications the lighthouse keeper had made to the small boat.

Mr. Eli know whut he doin,' he thought.

He did think of one improvement he could make to Eli's boat since he knew he would probably have it for another month or so. He could paint the gunnels haint blue. He wouldn't paint the whole boat, but bright blue trim would make the white boat more attractive. It would also give his friend Eli additional protection from anything that intended to do him harm.

With his powerful right arm, he pulled the skiff up onto the cypress dock.

Need hit to dry out 'fo' I paint.

The light in Maggie Howard's house came on. Samuel felt his heart beat at the thought of the beautiful Maggie. He hobbled back to his own place, climbed the stairs, and retrieved the ham given to him by Eli. He struggled back down the stairs and limped across the track to Maggie's door. Hesitantly he knocked.

When she opened the door, he was speechless for a moment. She had on the same faded cotton dress she had worn the night she held his arm. The dress only slightly concealed her shapely form.

She spoke first. "Ain't oonuh up early? Can't come in jest now. Wouldn't be proper. But oonuh still comin' to supper, I hope."

"Sho, am."

"I brung oonuh dis ham. Got hit from Mr. Eli out to de lighthouse. Thought oonuh might use it."

"We hab dat ham fo' supper wit' black-eyed peas and collards. Wished I'd had some taters."

"I might jest come up wit some."

"Brung 'em to me if'n oonuh do."

She tiptoed and kissed him on the cheek. "See oonuh tonight. Come hungry."

"Sho' will."

Samuel went straight back to the dock and put the skiff in the water. He could paint it later. Right now, he needed to find some sweet potatoes, and he knew just the place.

On this beautiful Christmas morning, he rowed the small boat toward Georgetown. The skiff handled well, responding to the oars.

Jest like plowin' a good mule, thought Samuel. *Know'd how to gee and haw.*

At the store, Samuel had no trouble opening the backdoor. Even when it was locked, he knew how to lift the door enough for the bolt in the lock to clear the keeper. He put three large sweet potatoes in his jacket pockets and closed the backdoor, making sure it was locked.

As he rowed back upriver, he paid attention to the sounds of Christmas morning. He heard the bells ringing at the Episcopal Church. He thought of the Catholic Church, the mayor, and the Christmas cigar he would enjoy later.

Further along on the opposite bank, a blue jay squawked from a water oak warning his kin of a large red-tailed hawk soaring above. In the distance, a noisy woodpecker hammered the dead snag of a yellow pine. Samuel had once seen an ivory-billed woodpecker at Greenfield, but just that once and never again. Though he couldn't see, the one he heard this Christmas morning was almost certainly a pileated with a Christmas-red head. Samuel called the large bird a hammerhead.

Back at his dock, he tied up the skiff. Painting the gunnels would have to wait. He walked slowly with his stick back to Maggie's house. She came to the door wearing an apron over the cotton dress. He presented the three sweet potatoes.

"Saw oonuh get in dat boat go down de riber. Where oonuh git dem taters?"

"Dug 'em up."

"Well, we'll have 'em fo supper. Now, don't oonuh be late."

Yes, ma'am. Ain't gonna' be late."

Maggie didn't kiss him this time, but she did wink at him.

There was no way Samuel would be late to supper. He went to his shanty and struggled up the stairs. Inside he found the piece of calico cloth he had cut just for this day. He wrapped the hand-carved doll in the red calico for Sally. He tore off the excess and wrapped the gold coin as a present for Maggie. He ate a small portion of beans, just enough to tide him over until supper.

Then he took the Cuban cigar the mayor had given him and sat down on the front porch. Samuel moistened the cigar with his own saliva and cut the end with his pocketknife. He struck a match and lit the fine tobacco. He took two deep draws on the cigar. It was a mighty fine smoke.

As he savored the Cuban tobacco, he thought about the people of Georgetown. Most folks got along together pretty well. This was home to many different kinds. Some, like his own kin, had been brought here against their will. Others had come by their own choice. Some had come a long time ago. Some, like Mr. Eli, had found Georgetown because one place or another had been cruel to them.

We jest all needs to git along.

For some, like Mr. Meade and Officer Holden, getting along was nearly impossible. They were ruled by fear, fear of anybody different from themselves.

Bad way to live, thought Samuel, *bad fo' dem and evuhbody else, too.*

Samuel smoked slowly, enjoying the taste and the aroma of the fine tobacco.

Jest like dis cigar. Some mighty good t'ings come from someplace else.

Mr. Kaminski, Mr. Eli, Miz Pringle, old man Jefferson — they all came from some other place. So did Samuel and all of his kin. But the same was true for Richard Meade and for Roy Holden. Everybody came from somewhere else.

It ain't so much where folks is from as 'tis how de treat each other. Dat what de Good Book say. Eben de Lawd hisself say dat in de Golden Rule.

Samuel heard a Carolina wren singing from the live oak. It sounded like a Christmas song to him. The gentle breeze carried the smell of baked ham wafting across the track from Maggie's house. Samuel finished his cigar. He walked to the marsh and discarded the butt in the pluff mud.

He drew water from the river in a five-gallon bucket and warmed it on his woodstove. Inside his house, he washed in a galvanized tub. He put on his only clean shirt and checked himself in the broken mirror. He was an old man. What in the world did Maggie see in him?

Just as he was headed over to Maggie's house, a car drove along the sandy road. It stopped in front of Samuel. It was Mayor Morgan.

"Hello, Samuel. Merry Christmas," the Mayor said.

"Yes, suh, Merry Christmas to oonuh."

"I thought I'd be by sooner. Hope I'm not too late."

"No, suh, not a' tall."

"Have you enjoyed that Cuban cigar yet?"

"Yes, suh. Mighty fine. Mighty fine."

"Here, have a couple more."

"Thank you, suh."

"And, I brought you a bag of fresh apples for Christmas."

"Why, much obliged, suh."

"I thought you might enjoy them."

"Sho' will."

"Samuel, you're a good man. Don't ever let anybody tell you different."

Samuel could hardly speak. Rarely had any white man said such a thing to him. Finally, he said, "T'ank oonuh, Mr. Morgan."

"Merry Christmas, Samuel."

"Same to oonuh, suh."

With that, the mayor drove away from the Gullah line. He watched as the one-handed mayor drove his big automobile back out the scrub board road and then turn onto the blacktop.

Still stunned by his conversation with the mayor, Samuel slowly made his way across the sandy track to Maggie's house. Maggie had a real house built by John. It had four rooms, including a front room, a kitchen, and two bedrooms, one for Sally and one for Maggie.

Samuel knocked on the door just once. Maggie welcomed him. She was barefooted but had on her Sunday dress. "Merry Christmas," she said. "Who was oonuh talkin' wit out dere."

"Mayor Morgan came by. He brung dese apples. Dey fo' oonuh."

"No such t'ing. I'll keep a few. Mabbe fix oonuh apple pie befo' long. Have a seat. Supper is nearly 'bout ready."

Samuel sat in the front room. Soon Sally came in to see him. She was a little child in a grown woman's body. She jabbered excitedly, but Samuel couldn't understand anything she said. "She jest glad to see oonuh," Maggie said from the kitchen.

Sally sat down by Samuel and played with his big gnarled hands. In a few minutes, Maggie called, "Y'all come on."

They went into the kitchen and sat down to the best-looking meal Samuel had seen since Rachel had died. "Look mighty good," he said.

"Sho hope so," responded Maggie.

"Will oonuh gib t'anks?"

Samuel bowed his head, "Lawd, make us thankful for all dy many blessings. Jesus' name. Amen."

Maggie served Sally and then Samuel. She loaded his plate full. "Dey say de way to a man's heart is thru his stomach."

"I reckon das one way."

"I got others, too. Savin' those for later."

Samuel ate his fill of ham, collards, black-eyed peas, sweet potato casserole, and homemade biscuits with molasses. After Maggie had cleared the dishes she brought out a pecan pie.

"I neber had it so good," Samuel said.

"Oonuh jest wait," said Maggie.

Samuel felt uneasy. Maggie and Rachel had been friends. Surely Maggie knew that he had lost his manhood. He wasn't sure what she had in mind, but there were just some things he couldn't do for a woman no matter how much he wanted to.

After supper, they gathered around the little Christmas tree Jasper had given him. Maggie and Sally had made all the decorations – paper chains, cut-out angels and stars, and one big paper star on top. Maggie read the Christmas story from the Good Book. Samuel was glad to know she could read so well. She asked him to pray.

Then they exchanged gifts. Samuel gave Sally the asafetida bag and the carved doll wrapped in red calico cloth. Maggie tied the bag around her daughter's neck to protect her from illness. Sally played with the doll and with the cloth. Maggie gave Samuel a gift wrapped in paper. It was a denim shirt, almost brand new, one that her late husband John had worn only one time.

Then Samuel gave Maggie the small gift wrapped in red calico. Her eyes lit up like a child's. "What? What 'tis?" she said excitedly. Carefully and slowly she opened the small present. When she saw the five-dollar gold piece, she shrieked, "Where? How? Oh, my Lawd, I ain't neber had nothin' so fine!"

"Miz Pringle gib it to me. I know'd right off I was gonna' gib it to oonuh."

She jumped to her feet and rushed to him, hugging his neck. She kissed his cheek and held him close.

Sally tried to get between them, but Maggie held Samuel tighter. After a minute she said, "I'm so happy to be wit oonuh."

"Me, too," said Samuel, and he shed a tear.

Samuel sat with Sally humming songs and telling stories. Maggie cleared the table, washed the dishes, and cleaned the kitchen. Then she put Sally to bed and told her the story about the baby Jesus.

When she came into the front room, she sat down by Samuel and took his arm as she had done on the front porch several nights before. She held him close, and he kissed her brow. Samuel wasn't sure what to expect. He had decided to let Maggie lead the way.

After a while, she said, "Know whut I wants?"

Whut dat?"

"I want oonuh to lay wit me."

Samuel didn't know what to say. Only the truth would do. After a moment, he spoke. "Maggie, eber since I got hurt at de lumber mill, dere's some t'ings …"

She interrupted, "I don't care 'bout whut oonuh can't do. Don't want to hear hit. I want oonuh to lay wit me and hold me and make me feel like a woman. Oonuh de only one who can do dat fo' me."

She took him by the hand, and he stood up. She kissed his cheek and led him to her bed. He closed the door leaving his walking stick propped against the wall in the front room.

Chapter Twenty-One

Professor Rosen:

Hanukkah, in the United States, features music and good food. Many traditional Hanukkah foods are cooked in oil, in remembrance of the oil that burned for eight days when the Temple was rededicated. In the United States, a favorite Hanukkah food is latkes or potato pancakes. This custom may have developed in Eastern Europe.

The final day of Hanukkah is a culmination of eight days of celebration. Hanukkah is one of the happiest Jewish events for many Jewish-Americans. Many families light candles in the menorah, enjoy a meal together, give gifts, and play with the dreidel, a spinning toy that is particularly popular during Hanukkah.

The last day of Hanukkah is the eighth day. It is the second day of the month of Tevet and marks the day on which the great miracle of oil concluded, according to traditional Jewish teaching. It is a particularly special day because it is the conclusion of the Hanukkah observance. The word Hanukkah means dedication. Many Jews regard the eight-day observance, sometimes called the Festival of Lights or the Feast of Dedication, as a time of personal commitment.

Tuesday, December 26, 1916 - The last full day of Hanukkah, North Island

Eli Solomon awoke to the sound of lovely music. Someone was singing in his own language. He recognized the tune as a lullaby from his native land.

He rolled out of his hammock and realized that for the first time in a long time, he had not had nightmares. Instead, he awakened to the sound of his daughter's voice, a song in the Ukrainian tongue and then in Yiddish.

Lenora had been up long before dawn. She wore an apron and had a colorful scarf tied over her long black hair. She had stoked the fire, now blazing brightly in the stove. She was scrambling guinea hen eggs for breakfast. Eli was so unaccustomed to having anyone to help that he hardly knew what to say.

"Thank you, Lenora."

"You are welcome, Papa."

"You know you don't have to do so much."

"Papa, I haven't come all this way to be a houseguest. I have come to be your daughter. We will live together as a family now. I will do my part."

She was so much like her mother – her appearance, her voice, her strength. Not only was he glad to be reunited with her, but he was also pleased with the woman she had become.

"I am so glad you are here. Thank you for helping."

She started singing again.

Eli went through the morning routine with renewed energy and joy. He could see that this unexpected intervention in his life had begun to change things for the better. Even the dog seemed livelier.

Over their meal, they had a lengthy conversation. She wanted to know how he became a lighthouse keeper. What was the daily routine on

North Island? How did he get to America? And how did he find his Uncle Mordecai?

Eli asked about her trip to find him. About her education. About her life. He was curious about how she survived the fire when she was an infant.

Speaking to him in Yiddish, she explained:

"Papa, I only know what I was told by the woman who kept me, Mrs. Prybilski. Her name was Sara. She said my mother was at home with me because you were at an important meeting at the synagogue to try to make peace in Odessa. My mother was feeling ill and asked if the neighbor could care for me until you returned home that evening. She said my mother had a fever and a rash. I was asleep at Mrs. Prybilski's house when the fire broke out.

"Mama Sara, as I called her, told me that she had tried to find you. I am not sure. Mama Sara was unable to have children of her own. I have often wondered if she just hid me so she could have a child.

"I learned less than a year ago, and entirely by accident, that you had gone to America to find your Uncle Mordecai. I wrote letters to you. The ones sent in care of Mordecai Solomon were returned undelivered. I wrote others to General Delivery. I guess you never got them.

"Once I became twenty-one, I told Mama Sara that it was time for me to find you. She was sad for me to leave. I was, too, but I had an unfinished sense about my life. I wanted to be with you, and I realized that you did not even know that I was alive.

255

"Things were not good for Jews in the Ukraine when I left, but Mrs. Prybilski had a younger brother who was a government official. He arranged papers for me to travel to Canada, and he generously paid for my trip.

"From Canada, I traveled to New York and booked passage to Georgetown, hoping that I might find you or at least find out what had become of you. Imagine my surprise when you appeared on the Meade family porch yesterday."

Tears came to Eli's eyes. "I don't have to imagine. I was never more surprised in all my life."

Father and daughter embraced as if they were seeing each other for the first time. Eli hugged his daughter and kissed her forehead. "But now we are together."

"I have so much to learn from you," said Lenora. "I am so glad to be with you. You will be my teacher."

"Perhaps," said Eli, "And you will teach me. I have much to learn from you, too."

With these words and this understanding, father and daughter struck a covenant with each other. The days and weeks ahead allowed them time to establish the bond for which each of them had hoped. At long last, it was time to be a family.

At sundown, with the steady beam of the Georgetown Lighthouse circling overhead, Eli and Lenora had supper together. Lenora prepared latkes with applesauce for her father. Following the meal, on the last evening of Hanukkah, they lit eight candles in the driftwood menorah in the window of the keeper's house on North Island. Lenora recited the prayers.

Blessed are You, Lord our God, King of the Universe,
who has sanctified us with His commandments
and commanded us to kindle the light of Hanukkah.
Blessed are You, Lord our God, King of the Universe,
who performed miracles for our fathers in those days and at this time.

She recited the prayers in perfect Hebrew.

Miracles, thought Eli, *in those days and at this time.*

Afterword

Professor Rosen, Hanukkah 1976, Temple Beth Elohim, Georgetown, South Carolina

When Professor Rosen finished her story, she brushed tears from her eyes, pushed a wisp of gray hair back from her wrinkled face, and said, "My name is Lenora Solomon Rosen. Eli Solomon was my father." She paused for a moment to collect herself.

"My father and I lived happily together on North Island. He always referred to our reunion as a miracle. We rarely saw Rupert. He had a way of showing up when we needed help of one kind or another.

"One week after the events related in my story, January 1, 1917, the dinghy from the *USLHS Cypress* washed ashore at high tide on the beach near the Coast Guard Station on Sullivan's Island near Charleston Harbor. The official report from the Coast Guard and the Lighthouse Service indicated that officer Roy Holden had left Georgetown Harbor alone in the small boat on December 22 in an impaired condition. He was presumed drowned at sea.

"I spent two years with my father on North Island. Those years were a happy time for both of us. Living on North Island was like living in paradise. I made a concerted effort to learn the English language.

"I arrived in December 1916. If I had waited just another few weeks, I would have never seen my father. In April 1917, the United States entered World War I. By October 1917, the Bolshevik Revolution had begun the slow transformation of the entirety of Eastern Europe into a Communist regime. My father and I were protected from these global events by the splendid isolation of North Island.

"The following year, something no less dangerous threatened us as well as millions of others. The influenza pandemic of 1918 was the deadliest in modern history. The flu virus infected an estimated 500 million people worldwide, about one-third of the earth's population. The flu killed an estimated 20 million to 50 million victims. More than 25 percent of the people of the United States became ill, and some 675,000 Americans died during the pandemic.

"My father was painting the dock one autumn afternoon. A fishing boat asked permission to tie up. One of the men on board was sick and in need of attention. My father asked me to prepare broth for the fisherman. After an hour or so, the sick man said he felt better. My father resumed his painting. Two days later, he came down with a headache, fatigue, and a fever. He had contracted influenza.

"After he had been ill with a high fever for several days, I knew I needed to get medical attention for him. I dared not try to take him to Georgetown in the skiff.

"When he did not go to Georgetown to purchase supplies, Samuel Pringle came to investigate. He took my father in his boat back to Georgetown. Maggie took care of him, but I stayed on North Island to maintain the lighthouse. Rupert came by to check on me every day. Though we couldn't converse with words, we managed to understand each other through a contrived sign language.

"A week later Samuel returned to get me and all of our possessions. My father had died. Eli Solomon was buried in the Jewish cemetery near his uncle's grave. His death was one of the 3000 fatalities in Georgetown County recorded in the influenza epidemic. Another was

Maggie Howard's daughter, Sally. Samuel was with Maggie to console her.

"Richard Meade lost the contract with the Lighthouse Service as a result of a dispute over a bill for a shotgun. The Lighthouse Service contended that Meade had falsified the invoice. Upon investigation of Meade's records and those of the Lighthouse Services, auditors discovered many such improprieties. The Lighthouse Service contract was awarded to Heiman Kaminski.

"Among many others, Richard Meade contracted the flu. At the time I was working as a waitress in Georgetown and living in a boardinghouse on Prince Street. Mrs. Meade came to me and asked if I would visit Richard at their home. I was surprised but agreed.

"When I arrived, Mrs. Meade insisted that I wear a covering over my mouth and nose. She ushered me to Richard's bedside. He was a very sick man and could barely speak. He spoke in a whisper. "I have a confession," he said. "The letters you wrote to your father came to my store. The writing was different. It was a different looking alphabet. I couldn't make sense out of the words. Rather than giving them to Eli, I destroyed them."

"You knew they were addressed to my father?"

After a long pause, he coughed and gasped for breath. "I did."

"Why?"

"I'm sorry," he whispered.

The following day Richard Meade died.

"My father died in October 1918, less than two years after I arrived in Georgetown, and we were reunited.

Immediately upon my father's death, the United States Lighthouse Service appointed a new keeper. If I had met him, there were many stories I might have told him. I never had that opportunity, and I have never returned to North Island. I did write a brief note to the new keeper, which I put inside *The Pink Book* explaining that he was the proud owner of a herd of Nubian goats, a flock of guinea fowl, and one very fine dog.

"Before I left Georgetown to pursue an education, I went to the Gullah Line to say farewell to Samuel Pringle. Under a live oak tree draped in Spanish moss, I found Samuel well and happy with his wife, Maggie. They were sitting together on a heart pine bench. The bench was painted haint blue."

De light dat shine een da daak,

an de daak ain't neba been able fa pit out dat light.

John 1:5

De Nyew Testament
Gullah Translation
American Bible Society,
New York, 2005

Resources and Bibliography

Georgetown County Public Library, Georgetown, SC.

Georgetown County Historical Society, Georgetown, SC.

Georgetown Museum, Georgetown, SC.

The Gullah Museum, Georgetown, SC.

The Maritime Museum, Georgetown, SC.

The Rice Museum, Georgetown, SC.

Allport, Gordon, *The Nature of Prejudice*, Addison-Wesley Publishing Company, Reading, MA, 1954.

Branch, Muriel Miller, *The Water Brought Us: The Story of Gullah-Speaking People*, Sandlapper Publishing Company, Inc. Columbia, South Carolina, 1995.

Cash, Wilbur J., *The Mind of the South*, Alfred J. Knopf, 1941.

De Nyew Testament, The Sea Island Translation Team with Wycliffe Bible Translators, American Bible Society, 2005.

Geraty, Virginia Mixson, *Gulluh Fuh Oonuh: A Guide to the Gullah Language*, Sandlapper Publishing Company, 1998.

Chandler, Genevieve Wilcox, Interviews conducted for the Federal Writer's Project of the Works Progress Administration in the 1930s.

The interviews are among the collections of the Library of Congress and the South Carolinian Library, University of South Carolina.

Instructions to Light-Keepers and Masters of Light-Vessels, 1902. The Pink Book issued by the United States Lighthouse Service (USLHS).

Joyner, Charles W., *Down by the Riverside: A South Carolina Slave Community*, University of Illinois Press: Urbana, 1985.

Lachicotte, Alberta Morel, *Georgetown Rice Plantations*, The State Commercial Printing Company. 1955.

Levitt, Theresa, *A Short Bright Flash: Augustin Fresnel and the Birth of the Modern Lighthouse*, W. W. Norton, 2013.

McAlister, Robert, *Georgetown's North Island: A History*, The History Press, 2015.

Peterkin, Genevieve C., *Heaven is a Beautiful Place: A Memoir of the South Carolina Coast*, University of South Carolina Press, 2000.

Pringle, Elizabeth Allston. *A Woman Rice Planter*, a later edition of the 1913 original, Southern Classics Series, University of South Carolina Press, 1992.

Pringle, Elizabeth Allston, *Chronicles of Chicora Wood*, a later reprint of the 1923 original, Cherokee Publishing Company, 2007.

Rogers, George C., *The History of Georgetown County, South Carolina*, University of South Carolina Press, 1970.

Author's Notes

December Light 1916 started life as a Christmas story. In 1996, my first year as pastor at Morningside Baptist Church in Spartanburg, South Carolina, I told a Christmas story instead of preaching a traditional sermon. On the last Sunday of Advent, I recounted the time when, as a ten-year-old, I played the part of Joseph in a children's Christmas pageant at Croft Baptist Church. It was an accurate account with gilded edges.

The Morningside congregation was delighted with the change in format. Several friends encouraged me to present a new story for Christmas every year. It was a daunting but exciting prospect. I did not have a new story for every year. I had only the old, old story, the one found in the Gospels. So, I wrote a new story each year, hoping to place the original Christmas story in a contemporary framework.

In subsequent years, on the Sunday before December 25, we removed the pulpit from the Sanctuary. We replaced it with a comfortable chair where I sat and shared an original Christmas story. Those stories were fiction, originating in my mind but based on real-life experiences. I believe that fiction is one of the best ways to tell the truth, especially the Gospel truth. Those Christmas stories were my gift to the congregation.

In December 2006, the Christian celebration of Christmas, according to the Gregorian calendar, overlapped with the Jewish observance of Hanukkah set by the Hebrew calendar. After a conversation with my friend Rabbi Yossi Liebowitz, I decided to write a story that would be suitable for both the congregation of Temple B'nai Israel and for the parishioners of Morningside Baptist Church.

I asked Yossi to read the story to correct any errors I might have made in describing the Jewish holiday. He made numerous suggestions which I incorporated into the writing. He liked the amended version of the tale so much that he invited me to present it as the sermon on the first night of Hanukkah 2006 at the Temple. The following Sunday, I offered it as the Christmas sermon at Morningside.

Over the next fifteen years, I continued to expand the story. I worked until it developed into a full-length novel.

Before I submitted *December Light 1916* for publication, I again asked Rabbi Liebowitz to read the manuscript. He made many helpful suggestions. Yossi and I discussed my decision to have the two antagonists – Richard Meade and Roy Holden – utter racial slurs against both African-Americans and Jews. *December Light 1916* is historical fiction. I have tried to tell the story being true to the culture of the Deep South in 1916. Racial slurs were part of that culture.

I intended to show that fear is the nature of prejudice and that people of integrity, regardless of their background and ethnicity, can make the world a better place by being true to that sense of integrity.

When I realized that I would need to create a narrator for the story to keep the tale from becoming historically dense, it was logical to make the speaker a Jewish scholar and to place the telling of the story in a synagogue during the season of light - Hanukkah.

To tell the story, I needed a lighthouse. The North Island Light near Georgetown was the prime choice because it was the last lighthouse in South Carolina to be automated. Until 1986 it was operated manually by a resident lighthouse keeper, ten years after the fictional Professor Rosen narrates this story in the bicentennial year.

The story had to be set in a time frame that met three requirements. I had to find a year in which Hanukkah and Christmas coincided. The story had to harken back to a time when the lamp in the lens was still fueled by lighthouse oil. I also needed a year when storms along the Southeastern Atlantic coast were numerous. 1916 met all three of those requirements.

In 1916 the beam of the light could be seen from Georgetown. That is no longer the case because the beam is weaker. In modern times, the Georgetown Light is rarely seen even by Georgetown residents. The lighthouse can only be seen from the air or from the water, a boat trip of thirteen miles from the Georgetown harbor.

When I first began researching the story, Wayne Wheeler, Past President of the United States Lighthouse Preservation Society, was an essential source of information. He is the one who described the lighthouse, the fourth-order Fresnel lens, and the clockwork mechanism that rotated the light.

The following day I was able to see the massive Fresnel lens at the Georgetown Coast Guard Station. The guardsman on duty that day confirmed the information that I had gleaned from Wayne Wheeler. That fourth-order lens was in place in 1916 and cast a rotating beam of eighteen miles.

In a 2014 conversation with Mac McAlister, a local Georgetown author and board member of the South Carolina Maritime Museum, he explained that the 1986 lens is now housed in the museum. It is a fifth-order Fresnel lens that did not rotate but held a steady beam.

So, I believe the fourth-order rotating lens in this novel is correct for 1916. Besides, this is a work of fiction that does not claim to be accurate in all historical details. It seems to me that the sweeping light of the fourth-order lens makes a much better story than the steady but weaker beam emitted by the fifth-order lens.

The location of the story in Georgetown was an appropriate setting for this tale. Because *December Light 1916* is a historical novel, I needed to learn the history of the area in the late nineteenth and early twentieth centuries to be reasonably accurate.

One thing I learned is that Georgetown was unique among Southern cities. Most folks in Georgetown tried hard to get along peacefully with each other. The Jewish community is a vital part of the life of Georgetown. The city has elected at least seven Jewish mayors. After the Civil War, a plan known as Fusion kept peace between Black and white citizens for nearly twenty years. While no place in the South was without discrimination, placing *December Light 1916* in the Georgetown milieu made perfect sense.

Though set in 1916, the story in this novel bears several similarities to our present time, 2020. Political disagreements over the issue of immigration are heated. Some contemporary politicians have even suggested that the words of Emma Lazarus from her "New Colossus" be removed from the Statue of Liberty.

> Give me your tired, your poor,
> Your huddled masses yearning to breathe free,
> The wretched refuse of your teeming shore.
> Send these, the homeless, tempest-tost to me,
> I lift my lamp beside the golden door!

Yet, it is precisely that national value that has guided immigration policy in the United States throughout our history. That is why Eli Solomon, in this novel, could come to this country, having escaped the pogroms in Ukraine, gain his citizenship, and become a lighthouse keeper.

In the Afterword, I included the deaths of three of the main characters caused by the Spanish Influenza epidemic of 1918. When I wrote that conclusion, little did I know that another deadly global pandemic, caused by COVID-19 would be sweeping this country and the world as *December Light 1916* was about to go to press in 2020. Readers will, no doubt, find other parallels between the time of Eli and Samuel and our own.

On a recent trip to Georgetown, my wife Clare and I were enjoying shrimp and grits in Thomas Café. As we talked about the town, the waterfront, and Winyah Bay, Clare said, "You really blur the lines between the fantasy of your story and the reality of Georgetown. You speak of Eli Solomon and Samuel Pringle as if they might clatter through the screen door and sit down with us at any moment."

I suppose that is the plight of any storyteller. The truth is that I have known Eli Solomon, not by that name, but in the experiences, I have had with people like him. I have stood in the surf of the Atlantic angling for bluefish with Eli. I have seen his patience and his persistence in that love relationship between hunter and prey that many do not understand. I have seen his anguish over matters of faith and his quiet life of devotion to that same faith. I have seen men like

Eli bury their grief in their work only to have it boil unbidden to the surface at inopportune times.

I have known Samuel Pringle in the men I have worked alongside at our family business, Neely Lumber Company, when I was growing up. At the lumberyard, I heard them speak with wisdom and insight in soft accents, much like Samuel's. I have listened to them sing, and pray, and talk about the women they love.

I have also seen the deep-seated fear and heard the vehement hatred in people like Roy Holden and Richard Meade. I have witnessed their same unrelenting racism and their seeming inability to grow past those stereotypes.

Clare is correct. These characters, while born of my imagination, are people with whom I have grown up. I know them very well.

The religious holidays of December share a message of hope. Hanukkah observance was intentionally set on the dark of the moon. The date for Christmas was placed near the winter solstice. People of faith in both the Jewish and the Christian traditions respond to the darkness with the wisdom of a Chinese proverb, "Better to light a candle than to curse the darkness."

These December holidays are times of sharp emotional contrasts. Many people are happy and have little difficulty finding joy in the season, but December brings sadness to others. For those who are hurting, these days may be filled with dread, despair, bitterness, and anger. Some are freshly wounded; others carry deep scars from years gone by. For them, this time is anything but "the season to be jolly." They suffer while others celebrate.

In fifty-four years of pastoral ministry, I have learned that there is no better way to present the message of hope that is at the heart of this season of light than through stories, and so, I have written my first novel, *December Light 1916*.

Faithfully,

Kirk H. Neely
Spartanburg, SC
July 2020

Acknowledgments

December Light 1916 is one of the Christmas stories I wrote for the Morningside congregation. As a novel, it has been in process for fifteen years.

I am grateful for the people of Morningside. Both the congregation of Temple B'nai Israel and the congregation of First Presbyterian Church, Spartanburg, have been faithful encouragers along the way to the completion of this book. Other congregations, some included in the dedication, have also given me a platform for storytelling through the years. Thank you all.

I am indebted to the work of other writers, especially George C. Rogers and Clarence C. Joyner.

Special thanks also to the Georgetown County Public Library, the Georgetown County Historical Society, the Georgetown County Museum, the Gullah Museum, and the South Carolina Maritime Museum.

The good people of Georgetown have been delightful encouragers. Walking on Front Street enjoying an ice cream cone, watching the boats and the boaters at the marina, riding out to the lighthouse with Captain Rod, and so many other encounters have helped me find this story in that storied old city. On a visit to the florist, I learned that the first Jewish Synagogue met upstairs above the jewelry shop. The owner of the florist shop rolled back the carpet and showed me the image of a diamond inlaid in the terrazzo floor. One day I walked to the cemetery, a quiet, serene place where I found graves of historical importance to the city. Though I was born and bred in the Upstate, I also feel right at home in the Lowcountry because of Georgetown.

Kathy Green, my Administrative Assistant at Morningside, and Didi Terry, my Administrative Assistant at First Presbyterian Church, have been a great help. Kathy typed, edited, and retyped the manuscript several times. Didi has cheered me on in the latter days of this work. Thank you both.

Holly Barnett was a student in my class, The Introduction to the New Testament, at the University of South Carolina Upstate. Toward the end of her last semester before graduation, she offered to become my *amanuensis*, my literary and artistic assistant. Not only have we spent many Saturday mornings video conferencing on ZOOM, but Holly also created the cover picture and the graphic artwork that illustrates these pages.

The inspiration for *December Light 1916* rolled in on the tides and blew in on the salty breezes of the Atlantic Ocean. For thirty-eight years, my family vacationed at Pawleys Island, sixteen miles north of Georgetown, in South Carolina. I have fished the surf, the inlets, and the tidal creeks. I have watched the sweetgrass basket makers ply their trade. I have listened to Gullah accents and heard the local lore. On many occasions, I have slept in a hammock. Once, on a foggy Sunday, I was mistaken, by my grandchildren, for the Gray Man, the benevolent ghost of Pawleys Island.

The writing muse, which may also be the Holy Spirit, has been my companion at the coast. I am sure it has something to do with removing my watch and living by the tides. A visitation is more likely when I step out of my shoes as Moses did at the burning bush. Once I declare a temporary media fast, I find that inspiration has a chance to get my attention.

These times of productive writing have been a gift to me from friends who own beach homes and are kind to offer them to us. *December Light 1916* was written overlooking the waterfront at a condominium in Georgetown Harbor and an oceanfront deck at North Myrtle Beach. The story was penned on legal pads on a backporch beside a canal on Kiawah Island, and on the front porch of beach homes at Edisto Island and especially, Pawleys Island. Thank you to our generous friends who gave us blessed retreats for this writing.

Sincere thanks to Todd Stephens and the staff of the Spartanburg County Public Library for the invaluable service they render to my family and me. We appreciate you in more ways than we can say.

I am grateful to Michael Curtis and Betsy Cox, who believed this story was worthy of publication and to Michel Stone, who hails from the Lowcountry. She read the manuscript and made many helpful suggestions.

I am thankful for members of a monthly book club at First Presbyterian Church, first started by my friend and colleague Bill Arthur. Following Bill's death, I was invited to lead the book club. His wife, Susanne, supported that transition and has remained a member of the club. These book club folks are friends who enjoy reading and talking together about the volumes we read.

David Russell Tullock is Executive Publisher of Parson's Porch Book Company. The first time I spoke with David, I knew we were kindred spirits. I knew that *December Light 1916* had finally found a home. Thank you, David, for publishing the book.

My friend and colleague, teacher, and confidant, Rabbi Yossi Leibowitz, has done so much to help with this effort, always being an encouraging presence and setting me straight on all things Jewish.

To nieces and nephews, to my students and congregants, and all who indulge my storytelling, I am grateful. Without you, I would be the only one laughing at my attempts at humor.

Our children and grandchildren are the people I have in mind when I write. I thank you, and I love each of you dearly.

To Clare, my wife of fifty-four years, my first and last editor, my best friend, my companion in all things, and the love of my life, thank you.

Kirk H. Neely
July 2020

About the Author

Kirk H. Neely was born in Spartanburg, South Carolina, in 1944. He is the oldest of eight children. He graduated from Spartanburg High School in 1962. Kirk received a Bachelor of Science degree in Biology and Chemistry from Furman University, Greenville, South Carolina (1966). He was licensed to the ministry by First Baptist Church, Taylors, South Carolina, in 1966. He was ordained to Pastoral Ministry by Crescent Hill Baptist Church, Louisville, Kentucky, in 1970. He received the Master of Divinity Degree (1970) and the Doctor of Ministry Degree in Pastoral Counseling (1973) from The Southern Baptist Theological Seminary, Louisville, Kentucky. He was named a Merrill Fellow at The Divinity School of Harvard University (1980), where he did postdoctoral study.

From 1973 until 1980, he was Pastor of Family Ministries at Knollwood Baptist Church, Winston-Salem, NC. From 1980 until 1996, he served as Associate Pastor of Family Ministries and Director of Pastoral Counseling Ministries at First Baptist Church, Spartanburg, SC. From 1996 until 2014, he served as Senior Pastor of Morningside Baptist Church, Spartanburg, SC.

Since 2012, Dr. Neely has served as an adjunct faculty member of the Religion Department of the University of South Carolina Upstate. In 2014, he was retained by First Presbyterian Church Spartanburg as a Pastoral Counselor. He also operates a private pastoral consultation service. In addition to teaching, counseling, and consultation, Dr. Neely is a freelance writer and a storyteller. He is a supply preacher and a retreat leader.

Dr. Neely is a frequent writer for the religion page of The Spartanburg *Herald-Journal*. From 2005 through 2019, he wrote a weekly column, "By the Way," for *H-J Weekly*. Currently, his "By the Way" column is published each week in the Sunday edition of the Spartanburg *Herald-Journal*. His articles have appeared in several other publications.

Kirk has a lifelong interest in promoting ecumenical and interfaith relationships.

Since his retirement as Senior Pastor of Morningside Baptist Church, Dr. Neely continues ministry through teaching classes in the Religion Department at the University of South Carolina Upstate, serving as Pastoral Counselor at First Presbyterian Church, Spartanburg, SC, and supply preaching in various churches. He has also continued his writing. *December Light 1916* is his debut novel.

Kirk and his wife, Clare, have been married since 1966. They are parents of five children and have thirteen grandchildren.

Dr. Neely may be contacted by e-mail at kirkhneely44@gmail.com for consultation or to schedule speaking engagements. You may consult his Website kirkhneely.com for a more detailed biography.